General Instruction of the Roman Missal

LITURGY DOCUMENTARY SERIES 2

United States Conference of Catholic Bishops • Washington, D.C.

Concordat cum originali:
    Msgr. James Patrick Moroney
    Executive Director, Secretariat for the Liturgy
    United States Conference of Catholic Bishops

The English translation of the *General Instruction of the Roman Missal (Third Typical Edition)* © 2002, International Committee on English in the Liturgy, Inc. All rights reserved.

Cover: Eyck, Jan van (c. 1390-1441). *The Adoration of the Lamb*, detail from the Ghent Altarpiece, 1432. Cathedral St. Bavo, Ghent, Belgium. Copyright Scala/Art Resource, N.Y.

First printing, April 2003
Third printing, October 2003

ISBN 1-57455-543-X

CONTENTS

CHAPTER III

The Duties and Ministries in the Mass 46

CHAPTER IV

The Different Forms of Celebrating Mass 53

Foreword to This Edition

The liturgical reforms of the Second Vatican Council have enjoyed great success in bringing many Catholics closer to the perfect sacrifice of praise that Christ the Lord offered from the wood of the Cross. Perhaps most of all, the reforms of the *Missale Romanum*, which regulates the celebration of the Eucharist as the "source and summit of the Christian life" (*Sacrosanctum Concilium*, no. 47), have been the cause and witness of this great work.

The first stages of the postconciliar reform of the Mass were marked by Pope Paul VI's apostolic constitution *Missale Romanum* (1969), which was quickly followed by the revised *Ordo Missae* (1970), including the first edition of the *Institutio Generalis Missalis Romani* (1970). This last document, which described the form for the new Order of Mass, was further revised in 1972 and yet more definitively as a part of the *editio typica altera* of the *Missale Romanum* on March 27, 1975.

After many years of preparation, the publication of an *editio typica tertia* of the *Missale Romanum* was authorized by Pope John Paul II in the course of the Jubilee Year of our Redemption and was published in spring 2001. This long-awaited revision includes a new edition of the *Institutio Generalis Missalis Romani*. On November 12, 2002, the Latin Church members of the United States Conference of Catholic Bishops approved a translation of the *Institutio Generalis Missalis Romani* prepared by the International Commission on English in the Liturgy. The translation was confirmed by the Congregation for Divine Worship and the Discipline of the Sacraments on March 17, 2003 (Prot. N. 2235/02/L).

The translation is published in this volume as a revision of the BCL Liturgy Documentary Series 2, which first appeared in 1970 and was intended to aid a common understanding of the first edition of the *Missale Romanum*. With the publication of the third edition of the *Missale Romanum*, the Bishops' Committee on the Liturgy (BCL) hopes that this publication of the *General Instruction of the Roman Missal* will assist with that same goal in our present day.

This revised *Institutio Generalis* possesses a unique role among all the documents on the liturgy. Like its preceding editions, it has been published in order to give life to a dream. It was the dream of reformers such as St. Hippolytus, St. Gregory, and St. Leo. It was the dream of Pope Paul VI and clearly remains the vision of Pope John Paul II, who calls us to "an ever deeper grasp of the liturgy of the Church, celebrated according to the current books and lived above all as a reality in the spiritual order" (*Vicesimus Quintus Annus*, 1988, no. 14). Likewise, this dream is shared by the Bishops' Committee on the Liturgy and the United States Conference of Catholic Bishops that it serves. Finally, it is the vision of the Church itself: the dream of God's people joined to Christ in Baptism and made "ever more holy by conscious, active, and fruitful participation in the mystery of the Eucharist" (*General Instruction of the Roman Missal*, no. 5).

Msgr. James P. Moroney
Executive Director
USCCB Secretariat for the Liturgy

GENERAL INSTRUCTION OF THE ROMAN MISSAL

Institutio Generalis Missalis Romani

Including Adaptations for the
Dioceses of the United States of America

CONGREGATION FOR DIVINE WORSHIP
AND THE DISCIPLINE OF THE SACRAMENTS

DECREE OF CONFIRMATION

Prot. N. 2235/02/L

THE UNITED STATES OF AMERICA

At the request of His Excellency, the Most Reverend Wilton D. Gregory, Bishop of Belleville, President of the Conference of Bishops of the United States of America, in a letter of November 13, 2002, and in virtue of the faculties granted to this Congregation by the Supreme Pontiff JOHN PAUL II, we gladly confirm and approve the English translation of the *Institutio Generalis Missalis Romani*, excerpted from the third typical edition of the same Missal, as in the attached copy.

Two copies of the printed text should be forwarded to this Congregation.

All things to the contrary notwithstanding.

From the offices of the Congregation for Divine Worship and the Discipline of the Sacraments, March 17, 2003.

✠ Francis Cardinal Arinze
Prefect

✠ Franciscus Pius Tamburrino
Archbishop-Secretary

UNITED STATES CONFERENCE OF CATHOLIC BISHOPS

DECREE OF PUBLICATION

In accord with the norms established by decree of the Sacred Congregation of Rites in *Cum, nostra ætate* (January 27, 1966), this edition of the *General Instruction of the Roman Missal* is declared to be the vernacular typical edition of the *Institutio Generalis Missalis Romani, editio typica tertia* in the dioceses of the United States of America, and is published by authority of the United States Conference of Catholic Bishops.

The *General Instruction of the Roman Missal* was canonically approved for use by the United States Conference of Catholic Bishops on November 12, 2002, and was subsequently confirmed by the Holy See by decree of the Congregation for Divine Worship and the Discipline of the Sacraments on March 17, 2003 (Prot. N. 2235/02/L).

Effective immediately, this translation of the *General Instruction of the Roman Missal* is the sole translation of the *Institutio Generalis Missalis Romani, editio typica tertia* for use in the dioceses of the United States of America.

Given at the General Secretariat of the United States Conference of Catholic Bishops, Washington, D.C., on March 19, 2003, the Feast of Saint Joseph, Husband of the Blessed Virgin Mary.

✠ Most Reverend Wilton D. Gregory
Bishop of Belleville
President
United States Conference of Catholic Bishops

Reverend Monsignor William P. Fay
General Secretary

Preamble

1. When he was about to celebrate with his disciples the Passover meal in which he instituted the sacrifice of his Body and Blood, Christ the Lord gave instructions that a large, furnished upper room should be prepared (Lk 22:12). The Church has always regarded this command as applying also to herself when she gives directions about the preparation of people's hearts and minds and of the places, rites, and texts for the celebration of the Most Holy Eucharist. The current norms, prescribed in keeping with the will of the Second Vatican Ecumenical Council, and the new Missal that the Church of the Roman Rite is to use from now on in the celebration of Mass are also evidence of the great concern of the Church, of her faith, and of her unchanged love for the great mystery of the Eucharist. They likewise bear witness to the Church's continuous and unbroken tradition, irrespective of the introduction of certain new features.

A Witness to Unchanged Faith
2. The sacrificial nature of the Mass, solemnly asserted by the Council of Trent in accordance with the Church's universal tradition,[1] was reaffirmed by the Second Vatican Council, which offered these significant words about the Mass: "At the Last Supper our Savior instituted the Eucharistic Sacrifice of his Body and Blood, by which he would perpetuate the Sacrifice of the Cross throughout the centuries until he

---

1   Ecumenical Council of Trent, Session 22, *Doctrina de ss. Missae sacrificio*, 17 September 1562 : *Enchiridion Symbolorum*, H. Denzinger and A. Schönmetzer, editors (editio XXXIII, Freiburg: Herder, 1965; hereafter, Denz-Schön), 1738-1759.

should come again, thus entrusting to the Church, his beloved Bride, the memorial of his death and resurrection."[2]

What the Council thus teaches is expressed constantly in the formulas of the Mass. This teaching, which is concisely expressed in the statement already contained in the ancient Sacramentary commonly known as the Leonine—"As often as the commemoration of this sacrifice is celebrated, the work of our redemption is carried out"[3]—is aptly and accurately developed in the Eucharistic Prayers. For in these prayers the priest, while he performs the commemoration, turns towards God, even in the name of the whole people, renders him thanks and offers the living and holy Sacrifice, namely, the Church's offering and the Victim by whose immolation God willed to be appeased;[4] and he prays that the Body and Blood of Christ may be a sacrifice acceptable to the Father and salvific for the whole world.[5]

In this new Missal, then, the Church's rule of prayer (*lex orandi*) corresponds to her perennial rule of belief (*lex credendi*), by which namely we are taught that the Sacrifice of the Cross and its sacramental renewal in the Mass, which Christ the Lord instituted at the Last Supper and commanded the Apostles to do in his memory, are one and the same, differing only in the manner of offering, and that consequently the Mass is at once a sacrifice of praise and thanksgiving, of propitiation and satisfaction.

---

2   Second Vatican Ecumenical Council, Constitution on the Sacred Liturgy, *Sacrosanctum Concilium*, no. 47; cf. Second Vatican Ecumenical Council, Dogmatic Constitution on the Church, *Lumen gentium*, nos. 3, 28; Second Vatican Ecumenical Council, Decree on the Ministry and Life of Priests, *Presbyterorum ordinis*, nos. 2, 4, 5.

3   Evening Mass of the Lord's Supper, prayer over the offerings. Cf. *Sacramentarium Veronense*, L. C. Mohlberg et al., editors (3rd edition, Rome, 1978), section I, no. 93.

4   Cf. Eucharistic Prayer III.

5   Cf. Eucharistic Prayer IV.

3. Moreover, the wondrous mystery of the Lord's real presence under the Eucharistic species, reaffirmed by the Second Vatican Council[6] and other documents of the Church's Magisterium[7] in the same sense and with the same words that the Council of Trent had proposed as a matter of faith,[8] is proclaimed in the celebration of Mass not only by means of the very words of consecration, by which Christ becomes present through transubstantiation, but also by that interior disposition and outward expression of supreme reverence and adoration in which the Eucharistic Liturgy is carried out. For the same reason the Christian people is drawn on Holy Thursday of the Lord's Supper, and on the solemnity of the Most Holy Body and Blood of Christ, to venerate this wonderful Sacrament by a special form of adoration.

4. Further, the nature of the ministerial priesthood proper to a Bishop and a priest, who offer the Sacrifice in the person of Christ and who preside over the gathering of the holy people, is evident in the form of the rite itself, by reason of the more prominent place and office of the priest. The meaning of this office is enunciated and explained clearly and at greater length in the Preface for the Chrism Mass on Holy Thursday, the day commemorating the institution of the priesthood. The Preface brings to light the conferral of the priestly power accomplished through the laying on of hands; and, by listing the various

---

6   Second Vatican Ecumenical Council, Constitution on the Sacred Liturgy, *Sacrosanctum Concilium*, nos. 7, 47; Decree on the Ministry and Life of Priests, *Presbyterorum ordinis*, nos. 5, 18.

7   Cf. Pius XII, Encyclical Letter *Humani generis*, 12 August 1950: *Acta Apostolicae Sedis*, Commentarium Officiale (Vatican City; hereafter, AAS), 42 (1950), pp. 570-571; Paul VI, Encyclical Letter *Mysterium fidei*, On the doctrine and worship of the Eucharist, 3 September 1965: AAS 57(1965), pp. 762-769; Paul VI, Solemn Profession of Faith, 30 June 1968, nos. 24-26: AAS 60 (1968), pp. 442-443; Sacred Congregation of Rites, Instruction *Eucharisticum mysterium*, On the worship of the Eucharist, 25 May 1967, nos. 3f, 9: AAS 59 (1967), pp. 543, 547.

8   Cf. Council of Trent, session 13, *Decretum de ss. Eucharistia*, 11 October 1551: Denz-Schön, 1635-1661.

duties, it describes that power, which is the continuation of the power of Christ the High Priest of the New Testament.

5. In addition, the nature of the ministerial priesthood also puts into its proper light another reality, which must indeed be highly regarded, namely, the royal priesthood of the faithful, whose spiritual sacrifice is brought to completeness through the ministry of the Bishop and the priests in union with the sacrifice of Christ, the one and only Mediator.[9] For the celebration of the Eucharist is an action of the whole Church, and in it each one should carry out solely but completely that which pertains to him or her, in virtue of the rank of each within the People of God. In this way greater consideration will also be given to some aspects of the celebration that have sometimes been accorded less attention in the course of time. For this people is the People of God, purchased by Christ's Blood, gathered together by the Lord, nourished by his word. It is a people called to bring to God the prayers of the entire human family, a people giving thanks in Christ for the mystery of salvation by offering his Sacrifice. Finally, it is a people made one by sharing in the Communion of Christ's Body and Blood. Though holy in its origin, this people nevertheless grows continually in holiness by its conscious, active, and fruitful participation in the mystery of the Eucharist.[10]

A Witness to Unbroken Tradition

6. In setting forth its instructions for the revision of the Order of Mass, the Second Vatican Council, using the same words as did St. Pius V in the Apostolic Constitution *Quo primum*, by which the Missal of Trent was promulgated in 1570, also ordered, among other things, that some

---

9   Cf. Second Vatican Ecumenical Council, Decree on the Ministry and Life of Priests, *Presbyterorum ordinis*, no. 2.

10   Cf. Second Vatican Ecumenical Council, Constitution on the Sacred Liturgy, *Sacrosanctum Concilium*, no. 11.

rites be restored "to the original norm of the holy Fathers."[11] From the fact that the same words are used it can be seen how both *Roman Missals*, although separated by four centuries, embrace one and the same tradition. Furthermore, if the inner elements of this tradition are reflected upon, it also becomes clear how outstandingly and felicitously the older *Roman Missal* is brought to fulfillment in the new.

7. In a difficult period when the Catholic faith on the sacrificial nature of the Mass, the ministerial priesthood, and the real and permanent presence of Christ under the Eucharistic species were placed at risk, St. Pius V was especially concerned with preserving the more recent tradition, then unjustly being assailed, introducing only very slight changes into the sacred rite. In fact, the Missal of 1570 differs very little from the very first printed edition of 1474, which in turn faithfully follows the Missal used at the time of Pope Innocent III. Moreover, even though manuscripts in the Vatican Library provided material for the emendation of some expressions, they by no means made it possible to inquire into "ancient and approved authors" farther back than the liturgical commentaries of the Middle Ages.

8. Today, on the other hand, countless learned studies have shed light on the "norm of the holy Fathers" which the revisers of the Missal of St. Pius V followed. For following the publication first of the Sacramentary known as the Gregorian in 1571, critical editions of other ancient Roman and Ambrosian Sacramentaries were published, often in book form, as were ancient Hispanic and Gallican liturgical books which brought to light numerous prayers of no slight spiritual excellence that had previously been unknown.

In a similar fashion, traditions dating back to the first centuries, before the formation of the rites of East and West, are better known today because of the discovery of so many liturgical documents.

---

11   Second Vatican Ecumenical Council, Constitution on the Sacred Liturgy, *Sacrosanctum Concilium*, no. 50.

Moreover, continuing progress in the study of the holy Fathers has also shed light upon the theology of the mystery of the Eucharist through the teachings of such illustrious Fathers of Christian antiquity as St. Irenaeus, St. Ambrose, St. Cyril of Jerusalem, and St. John Chrysostom.

9. For this reason, the "norm of the holy Fathers" requires not only the preservation of what our immediate forebears have passed on to us, but also an understanding and a more profound study of the Church's entire past and of all the ways in which her one and only faith has been set forth in the quite diverse human and social forms prevailing in the Semitic, Greek, and Latin areas. Moreover, this broader view allows us to see how the Holy Spirit endows the People of God with a marvelous fidelity in preserving the unalterable deposit of faith, even amid a very great variety of prayers and rites.

Accommodation to New Conditions
10. The new Missal, therefore, while bearing witness to the Roman Church's rule of prayer (*lex orandi*), also safeguards the deposit of faith handed down by the more recent Councils and marks in its own right a step of great importance in liturgical tradition.

Indeed, when the Fathers of the Second Vatican Council reaffirmed the dogmatic pronouncements of the Council of Trent, they spoke at a far different time in world history, so that they were able to bring forward proposals and measures of a pastoral nature that could not have even been foreseen four centuries earlier.

11. The Council of Trent already recognized the great catechetical value contained in the celebration of Mass but was unable to bring out all its consequences in regard to actual practice. In fact, many were pressing for permission to use the vernacular in celebrating the Eucharistic Sacrifice; but the Council, weighing the conditions of that age, considered it a duty to answer this request with a reaffirmation of the Church's traditional teaching, according to which the Eucharistic

Sacrifice is, first and foremost, the action of Christ himself, and therefore its proper efficacy is unaffected by the manner in which the faithful take part in it. The Council for this reason stated in firm but measured words, "Although the Mass contains much instruction for people of faith, nevertheless it did not seem expedient to the Fathers that it be celebrated everywhere in the vernacular."[12] The Council accordingly anathematized anyone maintaining that "the rite of the Roman Church, in which part of the Canon and the words of consecration are spoken in a low voice, is to be condemned, or that the Mass must be celebrated only in the vernacular."[13] Although on the one hand it prohibited the use of the vernacular in the Mass, nevertheless, on the other hand, the Council did direct pastors of souls to put appropriate catechesis in its place: "Lest Christ's flock go hungry . . . the Holy Synod commands pastors and all others having the care of souls to give frequent instructions during the celebration of Mass, either personally or through others, concerning what is read at Mass; among other things, they should include some explanation of the mystery of this most holy Sacrifice, especially on Sundays and holy days."[14]

12. Therefore, when the Second Vatican Council convened in order to accommodate the Church to the requirements of her proper apostolic office precisely in these times, it examined thoroughly, as had Trent, the instructive and pastoral character of the sacred Liturgy.[15] Since no Catholic would now deny the lawfulness and efficacy of a sacred rite celebrated in Latin, the Council was also able to grant that "the use of the vernacular language may frequently be of great advantage to the people"

---

12   Ecumenical Council of Trent, Session 22, *Doctrina de ss. Missae sacrificio*, 17 September 1562, chapter 8: Denz-Schön, 1749.

13   Ecumenical Council of Trent, Session 22, *Doctrina de ss. Missae sacrificio*, 17 September 1562, chapter 9: Denz-Schön, 1759.

14   Ecumenical Council of Trent, Session 22, *Doctrina de ss. Missae sacrificio*, 17 September 1562, chapter 8: Denz-Schön, 1749.

15   Cf. Second Vatican Ecumenical Council, Constitution on the Sacred Liturgy, *Sacrosanctum Concilium*, no. 33.

and gave the faculty for its use.[16] The enthusiasm in response to this meas-
ure has been so great everywhere that it has led, under the leadership of
the Bishops and the Apostolic See itself, to permission for all liturgical
celebrations in which the people participate to be in the vernacular, for
the sake of a better comprehension of the mystery being celebrated.

13. Indeed, since the use of the vernacular in the sacred Liturgy may certainly be considered an important means for presenting more clearly the
catechesis regarding the mystery that is inherent in the celebration itself,
the Second Vatican Council also ordered that certain prescriptions of
the Council of Trent that had not been followed everywhere be brought
to fruition, such as the homily to be given on Sundays and holy days[17]
and the faculty to interject certain explanations during the sacred rites
themselves.[18]

Above all, the Second Vatican Council, which urged "that more perfect
form of participation in the Mass by which the faithful, after the priest's
Communion, receive the Lord's Body from the same Sacrifice,"[19] called
for another desire of the Fathers of Trent to be realized, namely that for
the sake of a fuller participation in the holy Eucharist "the faithful present at each Mass should communicate not only by spiritual desire but
also by sacramental reception of the Eucharist."[20]

---

16   Cf. Second Vatican Ecumenical Council, Constitution on the Sacred Liturgy,
      Sacrosanctum Concilium, no. 36.
17   Cf. Second Vatican Ecumenical Council, Constitution on the Sacred Liturgy,
      Sacrosanctum Concilium, no. 52.
18   Cf. Second Vatican Ecumenical Council, Constitution on the Sacred Liturgy,
      Sacrosanctum Concilium, no. 35:3.
19   Second Vatican Ecumenical Council, Constitution on the Sacred Liturgy,
      Sacrosanctum Concilium, no. 55.
20   Ecumenical Council of Trent, Session 22, *Doctrina de ss. Missae sacrificio*, 17
      September 1562, chapter 6: Denz-Schön, 1747.

14. Moved by the same desire and pastoral concern, the Second Vatican Council was able to give renewed consideration to what was established by Trent on Communion under both kinds. And indeed, since no one today calls into doubt in any way the doctrinal principles on the complete efficacy of Eucharistic Communion under the species of bread alone, the Council thus gave permission for the reception of Communion under both kinds on some occasions, because this clearer form of the sacramental sign offers a particular opportunity of deepening the understanding of the mystery in which the faithful take part.[21]

15. In this manner the Church, while remaining faithful to her office as teacher of truth safeguarding "things old," that is, the deposit of tradition, fulfills at the same time another duty, that of examining and prudently bringing forth "things new" (cf. Mt 13:52).

Accordingly, a part of the new Missal directs the prayers of the Church in a more open way to the needs of our times, which is above all true of the Ritual Masses and the Masses for Various Needs, in which tradition and new elements are appropriately harmonized. Thus, while many expressions, drawn from the Church's most ancient tradition and familiar through the many editions of the *Roman Missal*, have remained unchanged, many other expressions have been accommodated to today's needs and circumstances. Still others, such as the prayers for the Church, the laity, the sanctification of human work, the community of all peoples, and certain needs proper to our era, have been newly composed, drawing on the thoughts and often the very phrasing of the recent documents of the Council.

---

21   Cf. Second Vatican Ecumenical Council, Constitution on the Sacred Liturgy, *Sacrosanctum Concilium*, no. 55.

Moreover, on account of the same attitude toward the new state of the present world, it seemed that in the use of texts from the most ancient tradition, so revered a treasure would in no way be harmed if some phrases were changed so that the style of language would be more in accord with the language of modern theology and would truly reflect the current discipline of the Church. Thus, not a few expressions bearing on the evaluation and use of the goods of the earth have been changed, as have also not a few allusions to a certain form of outward penance belonging to past ages of the Church.

Finally, in this manner the liturgical norms of the Council of Trent have certainly been completed and perfected in many respects by those of the Second Vatican Council, which has brought to realization the efforts of the last four hundred years to bring the faithful closer to the sacred Liturgy especially in recent times, and above all the zeal for the Liturgy promoted by St. Pius X and his successors.

CHAPTER I
The Importance and Dignity of the Eucharistic Celebration

16. The celebration of Mass, as the action of Christ and the People of God arrayed hierarchically, is the center of the whole Christian life for the Church both universal and local, as well as for each of the faithful individually.[22] In it is found the high point both of the action by which God sanctifies the world in Christ and of the worship that the human race offers to the Father, adoring him through Christ, the Son of God, in the Holy Spirit.[23] In it, moreover, during the course of the year, the mysteries of redemption are recalled so as in some way to be made present.[24] Furthermore, the other sacred actions and all the activities of the Christian life are bound up with it, flow from it, and are ordered to it.[25]

---

22   Cf. Second Vatican Ecumenical Council, Constitution on the Sacred Liturgy, *Sacrosanctum Concilium*, no. 41; Dogmatic Constitution on the Church, *Lumen gentium*, no. 11; Decree on the Ministry and Life of Priests, *Presbyterorum ordinis*, nos. 2, 5, 6; Decree on the Pastoral Office of Bishops, *Christus Dominus*, 28 October 1965, no. 30; Second Vatican Ecumenical Council, Decree on Ecumenism, *Unitatis redintegratio*, 21 November 1964, no. 15; Sacred Congregation of Rites, Instruction *Eucharisticum mysterium*, On the worship of the Eucharist, 25 May 1967, nos. 3e, 6: AAS 59 (1967), pp. 542, 544-545.

23   Cf. Second Vatican Ecumenical Council, Constitution on the Sacred Liturgy, *Sacrosanctum Concilium*, no. 10.

24   Cf. Second Vatican Ecumenical Council, Constitution on the Sacred Liturgy, *Sacrosanctum Concilium*, no. 102.

25   Cf. Second Vatican Ecumenical Council, Constitution on the Sacred Liturgy, *Sacrosanctum Concilium*, no. 10; cf. Decree on the Ministry and Life of Priests, *Presbyterorum ordinis*, no. 5.

17. It is therefore of the greatest importance that the celebration of the Mass—that is, the Lord's Supper—be so arranged that the sacred ministers and the faithful taking part in it, according to the proper state of each, may derive from it more abundantly[26] those fruits for the sake of which Christ the Lord instituted the Eucharistic Sacrifice of his Body and Blood and entrusted it to the Church, his beloved Bride, as the memorial of his Passion and Resurrection.[27]

18. This will best be accomplished if, with due regard for the nature and the particular circumstances of each liturgical assembly, the entire celebration is planned in such a way that it leads to a conscious, active, and full participation of the faithful both in body and in mind, a participation burning with faith, hope, and charity, of the sort which is desired by the Church and demanded by the very nature of the celebration, and to which the Christian people have a right and duty by reason of their Baptism.[28]

19. Even if it is sometimes not possible to have the presence and active participation of the faithful, which bring out more plainly the ecclesial nature of the celebration,[29] the Eucharistic Celebration always retains its efficacy and dignity because it is the action of Christ and the Church, in which the priest fulfills his own principal office and always acts for the people's salvation.

It is therefore recommended that the priest celebrate the Eucharistic Sacrifice even daily, if possible.[30]

---

26 Cf. Second Vatican Ecumenical Council, Constitution on the Sacred Liturgy, *Sacrosanctum Concilium*, nos. 14, 19, 26, 28, 30.

27 Cf. Second Vatican Ecumenical Council, Constitution on the Sacred Liturgy, *Sacrosanctum Concilium*, no. 47.

28 Cf. Second Vatican Ecumenical Council, Constitution on the Sacred Liturgy, *Sacrosanctum Concilium*, no. 14.

29 Cf. Second Vatican Ecumenical Council, Constitution on the Sacred Liturgy, *Sacrosanctum Concilium*, no. 41.

30 Cf. Second Vatican Ecumenical Council, Decree on the Ministry and Life of Priests, *Presbyterorum ordinis*, no. 13; *Codex Iuris Canonici*, can. 904.

20. Because, however, the celebration of the Eucharist, like the entire Liturgy, is carried out through perceptible signs that nourish, strengthen, and express faith,[31] the utmost care must be taken to choose and to arrange those forms and elements set forth by the Church that, in view of the circumstances of the people and the place, will more effectively foster active and full participation and more properly respond to the spiritual needs of the faithful.

21. This Instruction aims both to offer general guidelines for properly arranging the Celebration of the Eucharist and to set forth rules for ordering the various forms of celebration.[32]

22. The celebration of the Eucharist in a particular Church is of utmost importance.

For the diocesan Bishop, the chief steward of the mysteries of God in the particular Church entrusted to his care, is the moderator, promoter, and guardian of the whole of its liturgical life.[33] In celebrations at which the Bishop presides, and especially in the celebration of the Eucharist

---

31   Cf. Second Vatican Ecumenical Council, Constitution on the Sacred Liturgy, *Sacrosanctum Concilium*, no. 59.

32   Special celebrations of Mass should observe the guidelines established for them: For Masses with special groups, cf. Sacred Congregation for Divine Worship, Instruction *Actio pastoralis*, On Masses with special groups, 15 May 1969: AAS 61 (1969), pp. 806-811; for Masses with children, cf. Sacred Congregation for Divine Worship, *Directory for Masses with Children*, 1 November 1973: AAS 66 (1974), pp. 30-46; for the manner of joining the Hours of the Office with the Mass, cf. Sacred Congregation for Divine Worship, *General Instruction of the Liturgy of the Hours*, editio typica, 11 April 1971, *editio typica altera*, 7 April 1985, nos. 93-98; for the manner of joining certain blessings and the crowning of an image of the Blessed Virgin Mary with the Mass, cf. The Roman Ritual, *Book of Blessings*, editio typica, 1984, Introduction, no. 28; *Order of Crowning an Image of the Blessed Virgin Mary*, editio typica, 1981, nos. 10 and 14.

33   Cf. Second Vatican Ecumenical Council, Decree on the Pastoral Office of Bishops, *Christus Dominus*, no. 15; cf. also Constitution on the Sacred Liturgy, *Sacrosanctum Concilium*, no. 41.

led by the Bishop himself with the presbyterate, the deacons, and the people taking part, the mystery of the Church is revealed. For this reason, the solemn celebration of Masses of this sort must be an example for the entire diocese.

The Bishop should therefore be determined that the priests, the deacons, and the lay Christian faithful grasp ever more deeply the genuine meaning of the rites and liturgical texts, and thereby be led to an active and fruitful celebration of the Eucharist. To the same end, he should also be vigilant that the dignity of these celebrations be enhanced. In promoting this dignity, the beauty of the sacred place, of music, and of art should contribute as greatly as possible.

23. Moreover, in order that such a celebration may correspond more fully to the prescriptions and spirit of the sacred Liturgy, and also in order to increase its pastoral effectiveness, certain accommodations and adaptations are specified in this General Instruction and in the Order of Mass.

24. These adaptations consist for the most part in the choice of certain rites or texts, that is, of the chants, readings, prayers, explanations, and gestures which may respond better to the needs, preparation, and culture of the participants and which are entrusted to the priest celebrant. Nevertheless, the priest must remember that he is the servant of the sacred Liturgy and that he himself is not permitted, on his own initiative, to add, to remove, or to change anything in the celebration of Mass.[34]

---

34   Cf. Second Vatican Ecumenical Council, Constitution on the Sacred Liturgy, *Sacrosanctum Concilium*, no. 22.

25. In addition, certain adaptations are indicated in the proper place in the Missal and pertain respectively to the diocesan Bishop or to the Conference of Bishops, in accord with the *Constitution on the Sacred Liturgy*[35] (cf. nos. 387, 388-393).

26. As for variations and the more substantial adaptations in view of the traditions and culture of peoples and regions, to be introduced in accordance with article 40 of the *Constitution on the Sacred Liturgy* because of benefit or need, the norms set forth in the Instruction *On the Roman Liturgy and Inculturation*[36] and in nos. 395-399 are to be observed.

---

35   Cf. also Second Vatican Ecumenical Council, Constitution on the Sacred Liturgy, *Sacrosanctum Concilium*, nos 38, 40; Paul VI, Apostolic Constitution *Missale Romanum*.

36   Congregation for Divine Worship and the Discipline of the Sacraments, Instruction *Varietates legitimae*, 25 January 1994: AAS 87 (1995), pp. 288-314.

CHAPTER II
The Structure of the Mass, Its Elements and Its Parts

I. THE GENERAL STRUCTURE OF THE MASS

27. At Mass—that is, the Lord's Supper—the People of God is called together, with a priest presiding and acting in the person of Christ, to celebrate the memorial of the Lord, the Eucharistic Sacrifice.[37] For this reason Christ's promise applies in an outstanding way to such a local gathering of the holy Church: "Where two or three are gathered in my name, there am I in their midst" (Mt 18:20). For in the celebration of Mass, in which the Sacrifice of the Cross is perpetuated,[38] Christ is really present in the very liturgical assembly gathered in his name, in the person of the minister, in his word, and indeed substantially and continuously under the Eucharistic species.[39]

28. The Mass is made up, as it were, of two parts: the Liturgy of the Word and the Liturgy of the Eucharist. These, however, are so closely interconnected that they form but one single act of worship.[40] For in

---

37   Cf. Second Vatican Ecumenical Council, Decree on the Ministry and Life of Priests, *Presbyterorum ordinis*, no. 5; Constitution on the Sacred Liturgy, *Sacrosanctum Concilium*, no. 33.

38   Cf. Ecumenical Council of Trent, Session 22, *Doctrina de ss. Missae sacrificio*, 17 September 1562, chapter 1: Denz-Schön, 1740; Paul VI, Solemn Profession of Faith, 30 June 1968, no. 24: AAS 60 (1968), p. 442.

39   Cf. Second Vatican Ecumenical Council, Constitution on the Sacred Liturgy, *Sacrosanctum Concilium*, no. 7; Paul VI, Encyclical Letter *Mysterium fidei*, On the doctrine and worship of the Eucharist, 3 September 1965: AAS 57 (1965), p. 764; Sacred Congregation of Rites, Instruction *Eucharisticum mysterium*, On the worship of the Eucharist, 25 May 1967, no. 9: AAS 59 (1967), p. 547.

40   Cf. Second Vatican Ecumenical Council, Constitution on the Sacred Liturgy, *Sacrosanctum Concilium*, no. 56; Sacred Congregation of Rites, Instruction *Eucharisticum mysterium*, On the worship of the Eucharist, 25 May 1967, no. 3: AAS 59 (1967), p. 542.

the Mass the table both of God's word and of Christ's Body is prepared, from which the faithful may be instructed and refreshed.[41] There
are also certain rites that open and conclude the celebration.

II. THE DIFFERENT ELEMENTS OF THE MASS
Reading and Explaining the Word of God
29. When the Sacred Scriptures are read in the Church, God himself
speaks to his people, and Christ, present in his own word, proclaims
the Gospel.

Therefore, all must listen with reverence to the readings from God's
word, for they make up an element of greatest importance in the
Liturgy. Although in the readings from Sacred Scripture God's word is
addressed to all people of every era and is understandable to them, nevertheless, a fuller understanding and a greater effectiveness of the word
is fostered by a living commentary on the word, that is, the homily, as
part of the liturgical action.[42]

The Prayers and Other Parts Pertaining to the Priest
30. Among the parts assigned to the priest, the foremost is the Eucharistic
Prayer, which is the high point of the entire celebration. Next are the orations: that is to say, the collect, the prayer over the offerings, and the
prayer after Communion. These prayers are addressed to God in the
name of the entire holy people and all present, by the priest who presides
over the assembly in the person of Christ.[43] It is with good reason, therefore, that they are called the "presidential prayers."

---

41   Cf. Second Vatican Ecumenical Council, Constitution on the Sacred Liturgy,
     Sacrosanctum Concilium, nos. 48, 51; Second Vatican Ecumenical Council,
     Dogmatic Constitution on Divine Revelation, *Dei Verbum*, 18 November 1965,
     no. 21; Decree on the Ministry and Life of Priests, *Presbyterorum ordinis*, no. 4.
42   Cf. Second Vatican Ecumenical Council, Constitution on the Sacred Liturgy,
     Sacrosanctum Concilium, nos. 7, 33, 52.
43   Cf. Second Vatican Ecumenical Council, Constitution on the Sacred Liturgy,
     Sacrosanctum Concilium, no. 33.

31. It is also up to the priest, in the exercise of his office of presiding over the gathered assembly, to offer certain explanations that are foreseen in the rite itself. Where it is indicated in the rubrics, the celebrant is permitted to adapt them somewhat in order that they respond to the understanding of those participating. However, he should always take care to keep to the sense of the text given in the Missal and to express it succinctly. The presiding priest is also to direct the word of God and to impart the final blessing. In addition, he may give the faithful a very brief introduction to the Mass of the day (after the initial Greeting and before the Act of Penitence), to the Liturgy of the Word (before the readings), and to the Eucharistic Prayer (before the Preface), though never during the Eucharistic Prayer itself; he may also make concluding comments to the entire sacred action before the dismissal.

32. The nature of the "presidential" texts demands that they be spoken in a loud and clear voice and that everyone listen with attention.[44] Thus, while the priest is speaking these texts, there should be no other prayers or singing, and the organ or other musical instruments should be silent.

33. The priest, in fact, as the one who presides, prays in the name of the Church and of the assembled community; but at times he prays only in his own name, asking that he may exercise his ministry with greater attention and devotion. Prayers of this kind, which occur before the reading of the Gospel, at the Preparation of the Gifts, and also before and after the Communion of the priest, are said quietly.

The Other Formulas in the Celebration
34. Since the celebration of Mass by its nature has a "communitarian" character,[45] both the dialogues between the priest and the faithful

---

44   Cf. Sacred Congregation of Rites, Instruction *Musicam sacram*, On music in the Liturgy, 5 March 1967 , no. 14: AAS 59 (1967), p. 304.
45   Cf. Second Vatican Ecumenical Council, Constitution on the Sacred Liturgy, *Sacrosanctum Concilium*, nos. 26-27; Sacred Congregation of Rites, Instruction *Eucharisticum mysterium*, On the worship of the Eucharist, 25 May 1967, no. 3d: AAS 59 (1967), p. 542.

gathered together, and the acclamations are of great significance;[46] in fact, they are not simply outward signs of communal celebration but foster and bring about communion between priest and people.

35. The acclamations and the responses of the faithful to the priest's greetings and prayers constitute that level of active participation that the gathered faithful are to contribute in every form of the Mass, so that the action of the entire community may be clearly expressed and fostered.[47]

36. Other parts, very useful for expressing and fostering the faithful's active participation, that are assigned to the whole assembly that is called together include especially the Act of Penitence, the Profession of Faith, the Prayer of the Faithful, and the Lord's Prayer.

37. Finally, concerning the other formulas:

    a.   Some constitute an independent rite or act, such as the *Gloria*, the responsorial Psalm, the *Alleluia* and verse before the Gospel, the *Sanctus*, the Memorial Acclamation, and the *cantus post communionem* (song after communion);

    b.   Others accompany another rite, such as the chants at the Entrance, at the Offertory, at the fraction (*Agnus Dei*), and at Communion.

The Vocal Expression of the Different Texts

38. In texts that are to be spoken in a loud and clear voice, whether by the priest or the deacon, or by the lector, or by all, the tone of voice should correspond to the genre of the text itself, that is, depending upon whether it is a reading, a prayer, a commentary, an acclamation, or a sung text; the tone should also be suited to the form of celebration and

---

46   Cf. Second Vatican Ecumenical Council, Constitution on the Sacred Liturgy, *Sacrosanctum Concilium*, no. 30.

47   Cf. Sacred Congregation of Rites, Instruction *Musicam sacram*, On music in the Liturgy, 5 March 1967, no. 16a: AAS 59 (1967), p. 305.

to the solemnity of the gathering. Consideration should also be given to the idiom of different languages and the culture of different peoples.

In the rubrics and in the norms that follow, words such as "say" and "proclaim" are to be understood of both singing and reciting, according to the principles just stated above.

The Importance of Singing
39. The Christian faithful who gather together as one to await the Lord's coming are instructed by the Apostle Paul to sing together psalms, hymns, and spiritual songs (cf. Col 3:16). Singing is the sign of the heart's joy (cf. Acts 2:46). Thus St. Augustine says rightly, "Singing is for one who loves."[48] There is also the ancient proverb: "One who sings well prays twice."

40. Great importance should therefore be attached to the use of singing in the celebration of the Mass, with due consideration for the culture of the people and abilities of each liturgical assembly. Although it is not always necessary (e.g., in weekday Masses) to sing all the texts that are of themselves meant to be sung, every care should be taken that singing by the ministers and the people is not absent in celebrations that occur on Sundays and on holy days of obligation.

In the choosing of the parts actually to be sung, however, preference should be given to those that are of greater importance and especially to those to be sung by the priest or the deacon or the lector, with the people responding, or by the priest and people together.[49]

41. All other things being equal, Gregorian chant holds pride of place because it is proper to the Roman Liturgy. Other types of sacred music,

48　St. Augustine of Hippo, *Sermo* 336, 1: *Patrologiae cursus completus: Series latina*, J. P. Migne, editor, Paris, 1844-1855 (hereafter, PL), 38, 1472.
49　Cf. Sacred Congregation of Rites, Instruction *Musicam sacram*, On music in the Liturgy, 5 March 1967, nos. 7, 16: AAS 59 (1967), pp. 302, 305.

in particular polyphony, are in no way excluded, provided that they correspond to the spirit of the liturgical action and that they foster the participation of all the faithful.[50]

Since faithful from different countries come together ever more frequently, it is fitting that they know how to sing together at least some parts of the Ordinary of the Mass in Latin, especially the Creed and the Lord's Prayer, set to the simpler melodies.[51]

Movements and Posture
42. The gestures and posture of the priest, the deacon, and the ministers, as well as those of the people, ought to contribute to making the entire celebration resplendent with beauty and noble simplicity, so that the true and full meaning of the different parts of the celebration is evident and that the participation of all is fostered.[52] Therefore, attention should be paid to what is determined by this General Instruction and the traditional practice of the Roman Rite and to what serves the common spiritual good of the People of God, rather than private inclination or arbitrary choice.

A common posture, to be observed by all participants, is a sign of the unity of the members of the Christian community gathered for the sacred Liturgy: it both expresses and fosters the intention and spiritual attitude of the participants.

---

50   Cf. Second Vatican Ecumenical Council, Constitution on the Sacred Liturgy, *Sacrosanctum Concilium*, no. 116; cf. also Sacred Congregation of Rites, Instruction *Musicam sacram*, On music in the Liturgy, 5 March 1967, no. 30.

51   Cf. Second Vatican Ecumenical Council, Constitution on the Sacred Liturgy, *Sacrosanctum Concilium*, no. 54; Sacred Congregation of Rites, Instruction *Inter Oecumenici*, On the orderly carrying out of the Constitution on the Sacred Liturgy, 26 September 1964, no. 59: AAS 56 (1964), p. 891; Sacred Congregation of Rites, Instruction *Musicam sacram*, On music in the Liturgy, 5 March 1967, no. 47: AAS 59 (1967), p. 314.

52   Cf. Second Vatican Ecumenical Council, Constitution on the Sacred Liturgy, *Sacrosanctum Concilium*, nos. 30, 34; cf. also Sacred Congregation of Rites, Instruction *Musicam sacram*, On music in the Liturgy, 5 March 1967, no. 21.

43. The faithful should stand from the beginning of the Entrance chant, or while the priest approaches the altar, until the end of the collect; for the *Alleluia* chant before the Gospel; while the Gospel itself is proclaimed; during the Profession of Faith and the Prayer of the Faithful; from the invitation, *Orate, fratres* (*Pray, brethren*), before the prayer over the offerings until the end of Mass, except at the places indicated below.

They should, however, sit while the readings before the Gospel and the responsorial Psalm are proclaimed and for the homily and while the Preparation of the Gifts at the Offertory is taking place; and, as circumstances allow, they may sit or kneel while the period of sacred silence after Communion is observed.

In the dioceses of the United States of America, they should kneel beginning after the singing or recitation of the *Sanctus* until after the *Amen* of the Eucharistic Prayer, except when prevented on occasion by reasons of health, lack of space, the large number of people present, or some other good reason. Those who do not kneel ought to make a profound bow when the priest genuflects after the consecration. The faithful kneel after the *Agnus Dei* unless the diocesan Bishop determines otherwise.[53]

With a view to a uniformity in gestures and postures during one and the same celebration, the faithful should follow the directions which the deacon, lay minister, or priest gives according to whatever is indicated in the Missal.

44. Among gestures included are also actions and processions: of the priest going with the deacon and ministers to the altar; of the deacon carrying the Evangeliary or *Book of the Gospels* to the ambo before the proclamation of the Gospel; of the faithful presenting the gifts and

---

53   Cf. Second Vatican Ecumenical Council, Constitution on the Sacred Liturgy, *Sacrosanctum Concilium*, no. 40; Congregation for Divine Worship and the Discipline of the Sacraments, Instruction *Varietates legitimae*, 25 January 1994, no. 41: AAS 87 (1995), p. 304.

coming forward to receive Communion. It is appropriate that actions and processions of this sort be carried out with decorum while the chants proper to them occur, in keeping with the norms prescribed for each.

Silence

45. Sacred silence also, as part of the celebration, is to be observed at the designated times.[54] Its purpose, however, depends on the time it occurs in each part of the celebration. Thus within the Act of Penitence and again after the invitation to pray, all recollect themselves; but at the conclusion of a reading or the homily, all meditate briefly on what they have heard; then after Communion, they praise and pray to God in their hearts.

Even before the celebration itself, it is commendable that silence to be observed in the church, in the sacristy, in the vesting room, and in adjacent areas, so that all may dispose themselves to carry out the sacred action in a devout and fitting manner.

III. THE INDIVIDUAL PARTS OF THE MASS
A. The Introductory Rites

46. The rites preceding the Liturgy of the Word, namely the Entrance, Greeting, Act of Penitence, *Kyrie, Gloria,* and collect, have the character of a beginning, introduction, and preparation.

Their purpose is to ensure that the faithful who come together as one establish communion and dispose themselves to listen properly to God's word and to celebrate the Eucharist worthily.

In certain celebrations that are combined with Mass according to the norms of the liturgical books, the Introductory Rites are omitted or performed in a particular way.

---

54   Cf. Second Vatican Ecumenical Council, Constitution on the Sacred Liturgy, *Sacrosanctum Concilium*, no. 30; Sacred Congregation of Rites, Instruction *Musicam sacram*, On music in the Liturgy, 5 March 1967, no. 17: AAS 59 (1967), p. 305.

The Entrance

47. After the people have gathered, the Entrance chant begins as the priest enters with the deacon and ministers. The purpose of this chant is to open the celebration, foster the unity of those who have been gathered, introduce their thoughts to the mystery of the liturgical season or festivity, and accompany the procession of the priest and ministers.

48. The singing at this time is done either alternately by the choir and the people or in a similar way by the cantor and the people, or entirely by the people, or by the choir alone. In the dioceses of the United States of America there are four options for the Entrance Chant: (1) the antiphon from the *Roman Missal* or the Psalm from the *Roman Gradual* as set to music there or in another musical setting; (2) the seasonal antiphon and Psalm of the *Simple Gradual*; (3) a song from another collection of psalms and antiphons, approved by the Conference of Bishops or the diocesan Bishop, including psalms arranged in responsorial or metrical forms; (4) a suitable liturgical song similarly approved by the Conference of Bishops or the diocesan Bishop.[55]

If there is no singing at the entrance, the antiphon in the Missal is recited either by the faithful, or by some of them, or by a lector; otherwise, it is recited by the priest himself, who may even adapt it as an introductory explanation (cf. no. 31).

Greeting of the Altar and of the People Gathered Together

49. When they reach the sanctuary, the priest, the deacon, and the ministers reverence the altar with a profound bow.

As an expression of veneration, moreover, the priest and deacon then kiss the altar itself; as the occasion suggests, the priest also incenses the cross and the altar.

---

55   Cf. John Paul II, Apostolic Letter *Dies Domini*, 31 May 1998 , no. 50: AAS 90 (1998), p. 745.

50. When the Entrance chant is concluded, the priest stands at the chair and, together with the whole gathering, makes the Sign of the Cross. Then he signifies the presence of the Lord to the community gathered there by means of the Greeting. By this Greeting and the people's response, the mystery of the Church gathered together is made manifest.

After the greeting of the people, the priest, the deacon, or a lay minister may very briefly introduce the faithful to the Mass of the day.

The Act of Penitence
51. Then the priest invites those present to take part in the Act of Penitence, which, after a brief pause for silence, the entire community carries out through a formula of general confession. The rite concludes with the priest's absolution, which, however, lacks the efficacy of the Sacrament of Penance.

On Sundays, especially in the Season of Easter, in place of the customary Act of Penitence, from time to time the blessing and sprinkling of water to recall Baptism may take place.[56]

The Kyrie Eleison
52. After the Act of Penitence, the *Kyrie* is always begun, unless it has already been included as part of the Act of Penitence. Since it is a chant by which the faithful acclaim the Lord and implore his mercy, it is ordinarily done by all, that is, by the people and the choir or cantor having a part in it.

As a rule, each acclamation is sung or said twice, though it may be repeated several times, by reason of the character of the various languages, as well as of the artistry of the music or of other circumstances. When the *Kyrie* is sung as a part of the Act of Penitence, a trope may precede each acclamation.

---

56   Cf. *The Roman Missal*, Appendix II.

The Gloria

53. The *Gloria* is a very ancient and venerable hymn in which the Church, gathered together in the Holy Spirit, glorifies and entreats God the Father and the Lamb. The text of this hymn may not be replaced by any other text. The *Gloria* is intoned by the priest or, if appropriate, by a cantor or by the choir; but it is sung either by everyone together, or by the people alternately with the choir, or by the choir alone. If not sung, it is to be recited either by all together or by two parts of the congregation responding one to the other.

It is sung or said on Sundays outside the Seasons of Advent and Lent, on solemnities and feasts, and at special celebrations of a more solemn character.

The Collect

54. Next the priest invites the people to pray. All, together with the priest, observe a brief silence so that they may be conscious of the fact that they are in God's presence and may formulate their petitions mentally. Then the priest says the prayer which is customarily known as the collect and through which the character of the celebration is expressed. In accordance with the ancient tradition of the Church, the collect prayer is usually addressed to God the Father, through Christ, in the Holy Spirit,[57] and is concluded with a trinitarian ending, that is to say the longer ending, in the following manner:

- If the prayer is directed to the Father: *Per Dominum nostrum Iesum Christum Filium tuum, qui tecum vivit et regnat in unitate Spiritus Sancti, Deus, per omnia saecula saeculorum (Through our Lord, Jesus Christ, your Son, who lives and reigns with you and the Holy Spirit, one God, forever and ever);*

---

57   Cf. Tertullian, *Adversus Marcionem*, IV, 9: *Corpus Christianorum, Series latina*, Turnhout, Belgium, 1953- (hereafter, CCSL), 1, p. 560. PL 2, 376A; Origen, *Disputatio cum Heracleida*, no. 4, 24: *Sources chrétiennes*, H. deLubac et al., editors. (Paris, 1941-), p. 62; *Statuta Concilii Hipponensis Breviata*, 21: CCSL 149, p. 39.

- If it is directed to the Father, but the Son is mentioned at the end: *Qui tecum vivit et regnat in unitate Spiritus Sancti, Deus, per omnia saecula saeculorum* (*Who lives and reigns with you and the Holy spirit, one God, forever and ever*);
- If it is directed to the Son: *Qui vivis et regnas cum Deo Patre in unitate Spiritus Sancti, Deus, per omnia saecula saeculorum* (*You live and reign with God the Father in the unity of the Holy Spirit, one God, forever and ever*).

The people, uniting themselves to this entreaty, make the prayer their own with the acclamation, *Amen.*

There is always only one collect used in a Mass.

B. The Liturgy of the Word

55. The main part of the Liturgy of the Word is made up of the readings from Sacred Scripture together with the chants occurring between them. The homily, Profession of Faith, and Prayer of the Faithful, however, develop and conclude this part of the Mass. For in the readings, as explained by the homily, God speaks to his people,[58] opening up to them the mystery of redemption and salvation, and offering them spiritual nourishment; and Christ himself is present in the midst of the faithful through his word.[59] By their silence and singing the people make God's word their own, and they also affirm their adherence to it by means of the Profession of Faith. Finally, having been nourished by it, they pour out their petitions in the Prayer of the Faithful for the needs of the entire Church and for the salvation of the whole world.

---

58   Cf. Second Vatican Ecumenical Council, Constitution on the Sacred Liturgy, *Sacrosanctum Concilium*, no. 33.
59   Cf. Second Vatican Ecumenical Council, Constitution on the Sacred Liturgy, *Sacrosanctum Concilium*, no. 7.

Silence

56. The Liturgy of the Word is to be celebrated in such a way as to promote meditation, and so any sort of haste that hinders recollection must clearly be avoided. During the Liturgy of the Word, it is also appropriate to include brief periods of silence, accommodated to the gathered assembly, in which, at the prompting of the Holy Spirit, the word of God may be grasped by the heart and a response through prayer may be prepared. It may be appropriate to observe such periods of silence, for example, before the Liturgy of the Word itself begins, after the first and second reading, and lastly at the conclusion of the homily.[60]

The Biblical Readings

57. In the readings, the table of God's word is prepared for the faithful, and the riches of the Bible are opened to them.[61] Hence, it is preferable to maintain the arrangement of the biblical readings, by which light is shed on the unity of both Testaments and of salvation history. Moreover, it is unlawful to substitute other, non-biblical texts for the readings and responsorial Psalm, which contain the word of God.[62]

58. In the celebration of the Mass with a congregation, the readings are always proclaimed from the ambo.

59. By tradition, the function of proclaiming the readings is ministerial, not presidential. The readings, therefore, should be proclaimed by a lector, and the Gospel by a deacon or, in his absence, a priest other than the celebrant. If, however, a deacon or another priest is not present, the priest celebrant himself should read the Gospel. Further, if another suitable lector is also not present, then the priest celebrant should also proclaim the other readings.

---

60 Cf. *The Roman Missal, Lectionary for Mass, editio typica altera*, 1981, Introduction, no. 28.

61 Cf. Second Vatican Ecumenical Council, Constitution on the Sacred Liturgy, *Sacrosanctum Concilium*, no. 51.

62 Cf. John Paul II, Apostolic Letter *Vicesimus quintus annus*, 4 December 1988, no. 13: AAS 81 (1989), p. 910.

After each reading, whoever reads gives the acclamation, to which the gathered people reply, honoring the word of God that they have received in faith and with grateful hearts.

60. The reading of the Gospel is the high point of the Liturgy of the Word. The Liturgy itself teaches that great reverence is to be shown to it by setting it off from the other readings with special marks of honor: whether on the part of the minister appointed to proclaim it, who prepares himself by a blessing or prayer; or on the part of the faithful, who stand as they listen to it being read and through their acclamations acknowledge and confess Christ present and speaking to them; or by the very marks of reverence that are given to the *Book of the Gospels*.

The Responsorial Psalm
61. After the first reading comes the responsorial Psalm, which is an integral part of the Liturgy of the Word and holds great liturgical and pastoral importance, because it fosters meditation on the word of God.

The responsorial Psalm should correspond to each reading and should, as a rule, be taken from the Lectionary.

It is preferable that the responsorial Psalm be sung, at least as far as the people's response is concerned. Hence, the psalmist, or the cantor of the Psalm, sings the verses of the Psalm from the ambo or another suitable place. The entire congregation remains seated and listens but, as a rule, takes part by singing the response, except when the Psalm is sung straight through without a response. In order, however, that the people may be able to sing the Psalm response more readily, texts of some responses and Psalms have been chosen for the various seasons of the year or for the various categories of Saints. These may be used in place of the text corresponding to the reading whenever the Psalm is sung. If the Psalm cannot be sung, then it should be recited in such a way that it is particularly suited to fostering meditation on the word of God.

In the dioceses of the United States of America, the following may also be sung in place of the Psalm assigned in the *Lectionary for Mass*: either the proper or seasonal antiphon and Psalm from the *Lectionary*, as found either in the *Roman Gradual* or *Simple Gradual* or in another musical setting; or an antiphon and Psalm from another collection of the psalms and antiphons, including psalms arranged in metrical form, providing that they have been approved by the United States Conference of Catholic Bishops or the diocesan Bishop. Songs or hymns may not be used in place of the responsorial Psalm.

The Acclamation Before the Gospel
62. After the reading that immediately precedes the Gospel, the *Alleluia* or another chant indicated by the rubrics is sung, as required by the liturgical season. An acclamation of this kind constitutes a rite or act in itself, by which the assembly of the faithful welcomes and greets the Lord who is about to speak to it in the Gospel and professes its faith by means of the chant. It is sung by all while standing and is led by the choir or a cantor, being repeated if this is appropriate. The verse, however, is sung either by the choir or by the cantor.

a. The *Alleluia* is sung in every season other than Lent. The verses are taken from the Lectionary or the *Gradual*.
b. During Lent, in place of the *Alleluia*, the verse before the Gospel is sung, as indicated in the Lectionary. It is also permissible to sing another psalm or tract, as found in the *Gradual*.

63. When there is only one reading before the Gospel,

a. During a season when the *Alleluia* is to be said, either the *Alleluia* Psalm or the responsorial Psalm followed by the *Alleluia* with its verse may be used;
b. During the season when the *Alleluia* is not to be said, either the psalm and the verse before the Gospel or the psalm alone may be used;
c. The *Alleluia* or verse before the Gospel may be omitted if they are not sung.

64. The Sequence, which is optional except on Easter Sunday and on Pentecost Day, is sung before the *Alleluia*.

The Homily

65. The homily is part of the Liturgy and is strongly recommended,[63] for it is necessary for the nurturing of the Christian life. It should be an exposition of some aspect of the readings from Sacred Scripture or of another text from the Ordinary or from the Proper of the Mass of the day and should take into account both the mystery being celebrated and the particular needs of the listeners.[64]

66. The homily should ordinarily be given by the priest celebrant himself. He may entrust it to a concelebrating priest or occasionally, according to circumstances, to the deacon, but never to a lay person.[65] In particular cases and for a just cause, the homily may even be given by a Bishop or a priest who is present at the celebration but cannot concelebrate.

There is to be a homily on Sundays and holy days of obligation at all Masses that are celebrated with the participation of a congregation; it may not be omitted without a serious reason. It is recommended on other days, especially on the weekdays of Advent, Lent, and the Easter Season, as well as on other festive days and occasions when the people come to church in greater numbers.[66]

---

63   Cf. Second Vatican Ecumenical Council, Constitution on the Sacred Liturgy, *Sacrosanctum Concilium*, no. 52; *Codex Iuris Canonici*, can. 767 § 1.

64   Cf. Sacred Congregation of Rites, Instruction *Inter Oecumenici*, On the orderly carrying out of the Constitution on the Sacred Liturgy, 26 September 1964, no. 54: AAS 56 (1964), p. 890.

65   Cf. *Codex Iuris Canonici*, can. 767 § 1; Pontifical Commission for the Authentic Interpretation of the Code of Canon Law, response to *dubium* regarding can. 767 § 1: AAS 79 (1987), p. 1249; Interdicasterial Instruction on certain questions regarding the collaboration of the non-ordained faithful in the sacred ministry of priests, *Ecclesiae de mysterio*, 15 August 1997, art. 3: AAS 89 (1997), p. 864.

66   Cf. Sacred Congregation of Rites, Instruction *Inter Oecumenici*, On the orderly carrying out of the Constitution on the Sacred Liturgy, 26 September 1964, no. 53: AAS 56 (1964), p. 890.

After the homily a brief period of silence is appropriately observed.

The Profession of Faith
67. The purpose of the *Symbolum* or Profession of Faith, or Creed, is that the whole gathered people may respond to the word of God proclaimed in the readings taken from Sacred Scripture and explained in the homily and that they may also call to mind and confess the great mysteries of the faith by reciting the rule of faith in a formula approved for liturgical use, before these mysteries are celebrated in the Eucharist.

68. The Creed is to be sung or said by the priest together with the people on Sundays and solemnities. It may be said also at particular celebrations of a more solemn character.

If it is sung, it is begun by the priest or, if this is appropriate, by a cantor or by the choir. It is sung, however, either by all together or by the people alternating with the choir.

If not sung, it is to be recited by all together or by two parts of the assembly responding one to the other.

The Prayer of the Faithful
69. In the Prayer of the Faithful, the people respond in a certain way to the word of God which they have welcomed in faith and, exercising the office of their baptismal priesthood, offer prayers to God for the salvation of all. It is fitting that such a prayer be included, as a rule, in Masses celebrated with a congregation, so that petitions will be offered for the holy Church, for civil authorities, for those weighed down by various needs, for all men and women, and for the salvation of the whole world.[67]

70. As a rule, the series of intentions is to be

---

67   Cf. Second Vatican Ecumenical Council, Constitution on the Sacred Liturgy, *Sacrosanctum Concilium*, no. 53.

a. For the needs of the Church;
b. For public authorities and the salvation of the whole world;
c. For those burdened by any kind of difficulty;
d. For the local community.

Nevertheless, in a particular celebration, such as Confirmation, Marriage, or a Funeral, the series of intentions may reflect more closely the particular occasion.

71. It is for the priest celebrant to direct this prayer from the chair. He himself begins it with a brief introduction, by which he invites the faithful to pray, and likewise he concludes it with a prayer. The intentions announced should be sober, be composed freely but prudently, and be succinct, and they should express the prayer of the entire community.

The intentions are announced from the ambo or from another suitable place, by the deacon or by a cantor, a lector, or one of the lay faithful.[68]

The people, however, stand and give expression to their prayer either by an invocation said together after each intention or by praying in silence.

C. The Liturgy of the Eucharist

72. At the Last Supper Christ instituted the Paschal Sacrifice and banquet, by which the Sacrifice of the Cross is continuously made present in the Church whenever the priest, representing Christ the Lord, carries out what the Lord himself did and handed over to his disciples to be done in his memory.[69]

---

68   Cf. Sacred Congregation of Rites, Instruction *Inter Oecumenici*, On the orderly carrying out of the Constitution on the Sacred Liturgy, 26 September 1964, no. 56: AAS 56 (1964), p. 890.
69   Cf. Second Vatican Ecumenical Council, Constitution on the Sacred Liturgy, *Sacrosanctum Concilium*, no. 47; Sacred Congregation of Rites, Instruction *Eucharisticum mysterium*, On the worship of the Eucharist, 25 May 1967, no. 3a, b: AAS 59 (1967), pp. 540-541.

For Christ took the bread and the chalice and gave thanks; he broke the bread and gave it to his disciples, saying, "Take, eat, and drink: this is my Body; this is the cup of my Blood. Do this in memory of me." Accordingly, the Church has arranged the entire celebration of the Liturgy of the Eucharist in parts corresponding to precisely these words and actions of Christ:

1. At the Preparation of the Gifts, the bread and the wine with water are brought to the altar, the same elements that Christ took into his hands.
2. In the Eucharistic Prayer, thanks is given to God for the whole work of salvation, and the offerings become the Body and Blood of Christ.
3. Through the fraction and through Communion, the faithful, though they are many, receive from the one bread the Lord's Body and from the one chalice the Lord's Blood in the same way the Apostles received them from Christ's own hands.

The Preparation of the Gifts

73. At the beginning of the Liturgy of the Eucharist the gifts, which will become Christ's Body and Blood, are brought to the altar.

First, the altar, the Lord's table, which is the center of the whole Liturgy of the Eucharist,[70] is prepared by placing on it the corporal, purificator, Missal, and chalice (unless the chalice is prepared at the credence table).

The offerings are then brought forward. It is praiseworthy for the bread and wine to be presented by the faithful. They are then accepted at an appropriate place by the priest or the deacon and carried to the altar. Even

---

70   Cf. Sacred Congregation of Rites, Instruction *Inter Oecumenici*, On the orderly carrying out of the Constitution on the Sacred Liturgy, 26 September 1964, no. 91: AAS 56 (1964), p. 898; Sacred Congregation of Rites, Instruction *Eucharisticum mysterium*, On the worship of the Eucharist, 25 May 1967, no. 24: AAS 59 (1967), p. 554.

though the faithful no longer bring from their own possessions the bread and wine intended for the liturgy as in the past, nevertheless the rite of carrying up the offerings still retains its force and its spiritual significance.

It is well also that money or other gifts for the poor or for the Church, brought by the faithful or collected in the church, should be received. These are to be put in a suitable place but away from the Eucharistic table.

74. The procession bringing the gifts is accompanied by the Offertory chant (cf. no. 37b), which continues at least until the gifts have been placed on the altar. The norms on the manner of singing are the same as for the Entrance chant (cf. no. 48). Singing may always accompany the rite at the offertory, even when there is no procession with the gifts.

75. The bread and wine are placed on the altar by the priest to the accompaniment of the prescribed formulas. The priest may incense the gifts placed upon the altar and then incense the cross and the altar itself, so as to signify the Church's offering and prayer rising like incense in the sight of God. Next, the priest, because of his sacred ministry, and the people, by reason of their baptismal dignity, may be incensed by the deacon or another minister.

76. The priest then washes his hands at the side of the altar, a rite that is an expression of his desire for interior purification.

The Prayer over the Offerings
77. Once the offerings have been placed on the altar and the accompanying rites completed, the invitation to pray with the priest and the prayer over the offerings conclude the preparation of the gifts and prepare for the Eucharistic Prayer.

In the Mass, only one Prayer over the Offerings is said, and it ends with the shorter conclusion: *Per Christum Dominum nostrum* (*Through Christ our Lord*). If, however, the Son is mentioned at the end of this prayer, the conclusion is, *Qui vivit et regnat in saecula saeculorum* (*Who lives and reigns forever and ever*).

The people, uniting themselves to this entreaty, make the prayer their own with the acclamation, *Amen*.

The Eucharistic Prayer

78. Now the center and summit of the entire celebration begins: namely, the Eucharistic Prayer, that is, the prayer of thanksgiving and sanctification. The priest invites the people to lift up their hearts to the Lord in prayer and thanksgiving; he unites the congregation with himself in the prayer that he addresses in the name of the entire community to God the Father through Jesus Christ in the Holy Spirit. Furthermore, the meaning of the Prayer is that the entire congregation of the faithful should join itself with Christ in confessing the great deeds of God and in the offering of Sacrifice. The Eucharistic Prayer demands that all listen to it with reverence and in silence.

79. The chief elements making up the Eucharistic Prayer may be distinguished in this way:

a. *Thanksgiving* (expressed especially in the Preface): In which the priest, in the name of the entire holy people, glorifies God the Father and gives thanks for the whole work of salvation or for some special aspect of it that corresponds to the day, festivity, or season.

b. *Acclamation*: In which the whole congregation, joining with the heavenly powers, sings the *Sanctus*. This acclamation, which is part of the Eucharistic Prayer itself, is sung or said by all the people with the priest.

c. *Epiclesis*: In which, by means of particular invocations, the Church implores the power of the Holy Spirit that the gifts offered by human hands be consecrated, that is, become Christ's Body and Blood, and that the spotless Victim to be received in Communion be for the salvation of those who will partake of it.

d. *Institution narrative and consecration*: In which, by means of words and actions of Christ, the Sacrifice is carried out which Christ himself instituted at the Last Supper, when he offered his Body and Blood under the species of bread and wine, gave them to his Apostles to eat and drink, and left them the command to perpetuate this same mystery.

e. *Anamnesis*: In which the Church, fulfilling the command that she received from Christ the Lord through the Apostles, keeps the memorial of Christ, recalling especially his blessed Passion, glorious Resurrection, and Ascension into heaven.

f. *Offering*: By which, in this very memorial, the Church—and in particular the Church here and now gathered—offers in the Holy Spirit the spotless Victim to the Father. The Church's intention, however, is that the faithful not only offer this spotless Victim but also learn to offer themselves,[71] and so day by day to be consummated, through Christ the Mediator, into unity with God and with each other, so that at last God may be all in all.[72]

g. *Intercessions*: By which expression is given to the fact that the Eucharist is celebrated in communion with the entire Church, of heaven as well as of earth, and that the offering is made for her and for all her members, living and dead, who have been called to participate in the redemption and the salvation purchased by Christ's Body and Blood.

h. *Final doxology*: By which the glorification of God is expressed and which is confirmed and concluded by the people's acclamation, *Amen*.

---

71 Cf. Second Vatican Ecumenical Council, Constitution on the Sacred Liturgy, *Sacrosanctum Concilium*, no. 48; Sacred Congregation of Rites, Instruction *Eucharisticum mysterium*, On the worship of the Eucharist, 25 May 1967, no. 12: AAS 59 (1967), pp. 548-549.

72 Cf. Second Vatican Ecumenical Council, Constitution on the Sacred Liturgy, *Sacrosanctum Concilium*, no. 48; Decree on the Ministry and Life of Priests, *Presbyterorum ordinis*, no. 5; Sacred Congregation of Rites, Instruction *Eucharisticum mysterium*, On the worship of the Eucharist, 25 May 1967, no. 12: AAS 59 (1967), pp. 548-549.

The Communion Rite

80. Since the Eucharistic Celebration is the Paschal Banquet, it is desirable that in keeping with the Lord's command, his Body and Blood should be received as spiritual food by the faithful who are properly disposed. This is the sense of the fraction and the other preparatory rites by which the faithful are led directly to Communion.

The Lord's Prayer

81. In the Lord's Prayer a petition is made for daily food, which for Christians means preeminently the Eucharistic bread, and also for purification from sin, so that what is holy may, in fact, be given to those who are holy. The priest says the invitation to the prayer, and all the faithful say it with him; the priest alone adds the embolism, which the people conclude with a doxology. The embolism, enlarging upon the last petition of the Lord's Prayer itself, begs deliverance from the power of evil for the entire community of the faithful.

The invitation, the Prayer itself, the embolism, and the doxology by which the people conclude these things are sung or said aloud.

The Rite of Peace

82. The Rite of Peace follows, by which the Church asks for peace and unity for herself and for the whole human family, and the faithful express to each other their ecclesial communion and mutual charity before communicating in the Sacrament.

As for the sign of peace to be given, the manner is to be established by Conferences of Bishops in accordance with the culture and customs of the peoples. It is, however, appropriate that each person offer the sign of peace only to those who are nearest and in a sober manner.

The Fraction

83. The priest breaks the Eucharistic Bread, assisted, if the case calls for it, by the deacon or a concelebrant. Christ's gesture of breaking bread at the Last Supper, which gave the entire Eucharistic Action its name in apostolic times, signifies that the many faithful are made one body (1 Cor 10:17) by

receiving Communion from the one Bread of Life which is Christ, who died and rose for the salvation of the world. The fraction or breaking of bread is begun after the sign of peace and is carried out with proper reverence, though it should not be unnecessarily prolonged, nor should it be accorded undue importance. This rite is reserved to the priest and the deacon.

The priest breaks the Bread and puts a piece of the host into the chalice to signify the unity of the Body and Blood of the Lord in the work of salvation, namely, of the living and glorious Body of Jesus Christ. The supplication *Agnus Dei*, is, as a rule, sung by the choir or cantor with the congregation responding; or it is, at least, recited aloud. This invocation accompanies the fraction and, for this reason, may be repeated as many times as necessary until the rite has reached its conclusion, the last time ending with the words *dona nobis pacem (grant us peace)*.

Communion

84. The priest prepares himself by a prayer, said quietly, that he may fruitfully receive Christ's Body and Blood. The faithful do the same, praying silently.

The priest next shows the faithful the Eucharistic Bread, holding it above the paten or above the chalice, and invites them to the banquet of Christ. Along with the faithful, he then makes an act of humility using the prescribed words taken from the Gospels.

85. It is most desirable that the faithful, just as the priest himself is bound to do, receive the Lord's Body from hosts consecrated at the same Mass and that, in the instances when it is permitted, they partake of the chalice (cf. no. 283), so that even by means of the signs Communion will stand out more clearly as a participation in the sacrifice actually being celebrated.[73]

---

73   Cf. Sacred Congregation of Rites, Instruction *Eucharisticum mysterium*, On the worship of the Eucharist, 25 May 1967, nos. 31, 32; Sacred Congregation for the Discipline of the Sacraments, Instruction *Immensae caritatis*, 29 January 1973, no. 2: AAS 65 (1973), pp. 267-268.

86. While the priest is receiving the Sacrament, the Communion chant is begun. Its purpose is to express the communicants' union in spirit by means of the unity of their voices, to show joy of heart, and to highlight more clearly the "communitarian" nature of the procession to receive Communion. The singing is continued for as long as the Sacrament is being administered to the faithful.[74] If, however, there is to be a hymn after Communion, the Communion chant should be ended in a timely manner.

Care should be taken that singers, too, can receive Communion with ease.

87. In the dioceses of the United States of America there are four options for the Communion chant: (1) the antiphon from the *Roman Missal* or the Psalm from the *Roman Gradual* as set to music there or in another musical setting; (2) the seasonal antiphon and Psalm of the *Simple Gradual*; (3) a song from another collection of psalms and antiphons, approved by the United States Conference of Catholic Bishops or the diocesan Bishop, including psalms arranged in responsorial or metrical forms; (4) a suitable liturgical song chosen in accordance with no. 86. This is sung either by the choir alone or by the choir or cantor with the people.

If there is no singing, however, the Communion antiphon found in the Missal may be recited either by the faithful, or by some of them, or by a lector. Otherwise the priest himself says it after he has received Communion and before he distributes Communion to the faithful.

88. When the distribution of Communion is finished, as circumstances suggest, the priest and faithful spend some time praying privately. If desired, a psalm or other canticle of praise or a hymn may also be sung by the entire congregation.

---

74   Cf. Sacred Congregation for the Sacraments and Divine Worship, Instruction *Inaestimabile donum*, 3 April 1980, no. 17: AAS 72 (1980), p. 338.

89. To bring to completion the prayer of the People of God, and also to conclude the entire Communion Rite, the priest says the Prayer after Communion, in which he prays for the fruits of the mystery just celebrated.

In the Mass only one prayer after Communion is said, which ends with a shorter conclusion; that is,

- If the prayer is directed to the Father: *Per Christum Dominum nostrum* (*Through Christ our Lord*);
- If it is directed to the Father, but the Son is mentioned at the end: *Qui vivit et regnat in saecula saeculorum* (*Who lives and reigns forever and ever*);
- If it is directed to the Son: *Qui vivis et regnas in saecula saeculorum* (*You live and reign forever and ever*).

The people make the prayer their own by the acclamation, *Amen*.

D. The Concluding Rites

90. The concluding rites consist of

a. Brief announcements, if they are necessary;
b. The priest's greeting and blessing, which on certain days and occasions is enriched and expressed in the prayer over the People or another more solemn formula;
c. The dismissal of the people by the deacon or the priest, so that each may go out to do good works, praising and blessing God;
d. The kissing of the altar by the priest and the deacon, followed by a profound bow to the altar by the priest, the deacon, and the other ministers.

CHAPTER III
The Duties and Ministries in the Mass

91. The Eucharistic celebration is an action of Christ and the Church, namely, the holy people united and ordered under the Bishop. It therefore pertains to the whole Body of the Church, manifests it, and has its effect upon it. It also affects the individual members of the Church in different ways, according to their different orders, offices, and actual participation.[75] In this way, the Christian people, "a chosen race, a royal priesthood, a holy nation, God's own people," expresses its cohesion and its hierarchical ordering.[76] All, therefore, whether they are ordained ministers or lay Christian faithful, in fulfilling their office or their duty, should carry out solely but completely that which pertains to them.[77]

I. THE DUTIES OF THOSE IN HOLY ORDERS

92. Every legitimate celebration of the Eucharist is directed by the Bishop, either in person or through priests who are his helpers.[78]

Whenever the Bishop is present at a Mass where the people are gathered, it is most fitting that he himself celebrate the Eucharist and associate

---

75   Cf. Second Vatican Ecumenical Council, Constitution on the Sacred Liturgy, *Sacrosanctum Concilium*, no. 26.
76   Cf. Second Vatican Ecumenical Council, Constitution on the Sacred Liturgy, *Sacrosanctum Concilium*, no. 14.
77   Cf. Second Vatican Ecumenical Council, Constitution on the Sacred Liturgy, *Sacrosanctum Concilium*, no. 28.
78   Cf. Second Vatican Ecumenical Council, Dogmatic Constitution on the Church, *Lumen gentium*, nos. 26, 28; Constitution on the Sacred Liturgy, *Sacrosanctum Concilium*, no. 42.

priests with himself as concelebrants in the sacred action. This is done not to add external solemnity to the rite, but to express in a clearer light the mystery of the Church, "the sacrament of unity."[79]

Even if the Bishop does not celebrate the Eucharist but has assigned someone else to do this, it is appropriate that he should preside over the Liturgy of the Word, wearing the pectoral cross, stole, and cope over an alb, and that he give the blessing at the end of Mass.[80]

93. A priest also, who possesses within the Church the power of Holy Orders to offer sacrifice in the person of Christ,[81] stands for this reason at the head of the faithful people gathered together here and now, presides over their prayer, proclaims the message of salvation to them, associates the people with himself in the offering of sacrifice through Christ in the Holy Spirit to God the Father, gives his brothers and sisters the Bread of eternal life, and partakes of it with them. When he celebrates the Eucharist, therefore, he must serve God and the people with dignity and humility, and by his bearing and by the way he says the divine words he must convey to the faithful the living presence of Christ.

94. After the priest, the deacon, in virtue of the sacred ordination he has received, holds first place among those who minister in the Eucharistic Celebration. For the sacred Order of the diaconate has been held in high honor in the Church even from the time of the Apostles.[82] At Mass the deacon has his own part in proclaiming the Gospel, in preaching God's

---

79   Cf. Second Vatican Ecumenical Council, Constitution on the Sacred Liturgy, *Sacrosanctum Concilium*, no. 26.

80   Cf. *Caeremoniale Episcoporum, editio typica*, 1984, nos. 175-186.

81   Cf. Second Vatican Ecumenical Council, Dogmatic Constitution on the Church, *Lumen gentium*, no. 28; Decree on the Ministry and Life of Priests, *Presbyterorum ordinis*, no. 2.

82   Cf. Paul VI, Apostolic Letter *Sacrum diaconatus ordinem*, 18 June 1967: AAS 59 (1967), pp. 697-704; The Roman Pontifical, *Rites of Ordination of a Bishop, of Priests, and of Deacons, editio typica altera*, 1989, no. 173.

word from time to time, in announcing the intentions of the Prayer of the Faithful, in ministering to the priest, in preparing the altar and serving the celebration of the Sacrifice, in distributing the Eucharist to the faithful, especially under the species of wine, and sometimes in giving directions regarding the people's gestures and posture.

II. THE DUTIES OF THE PEOPLE OF GOD

95. In the celebration of Mass the faithful form a holy people, a people whom God has made his own, a royal priesthood, so that they may give thanks to God and offer the spotless Victim not only through the hands of the priest but also together with him, and so that they may learn to offer themselves.[83] They should, moreover, endeavor to make this clear by their deep religious sense and their charity toward brothers and sisters who participate with them in the same celebration.

Thus, they are to shun any appearance of individualism or division, keeping before their eyes that they have only one Father in heaven and accordingly are all brothers and sisters to each other.

96. Indeed, they form one body, whether by hearing the word of God, or by joining in the prayers and the singing, or above all by the common offering of Sacrifice and by a common partaking at the Lord's table. This unity is beautifully apparent from the gestures and postures observed in common by the faithful.

97. The faithful, moreover, should not refuse to serve the People of God gladly whenever they are asked to perform some particular ministry or function in the celebration.

---

83   Cf. Second Vatican Ecumenical Council, Constitution on the Sacred Liturgy, *Sacrosanctum Concilium*, no. 48; Sacred Congregation of Rites, Instruction *Eucharisticum mysterium*, On the worship of the Eucharist, 25 May 1967, no. 12: AAS 59 (1967), pp. 548-549.

III. PARTICULAR MINISTRIES

The Ministry of the Instituted Acolyte and Lector
98. The acolyte is instituted to serve at the altar and to assist the priest and deacon. In particular, it is his responsibility to prepare the altar and the sacred vessels and, if it is necessary, as an extraordinary minister, to distribute the Eucharist to the faithful.[84]

In the ministry of the altar, the acolyte has his own functions (cf. nos. 187-193), which he must perform personally.

99. The lector is instituted to proclaim the readings from Sacred Scripture, with the exception of the Gospel. He may also announce the intentions for the Prayer of the Faithful and, in the absence of a psalmist, proclaim the Psalm between the readings.

In the Eucharistic Celebration, the lector has his own proper office (cf. nos. 194-198), which he must exercise personally.

Other Ministries
100. In the absence of an instituted acolyte, lay ministers may be deputed to serve at the altar and assist the priest and the deacon; they may carry the cross, the candles, the thurible, the bread, the wine, and the water, and they may also be deputed to distribute Holy Communion as extraordinary ministers.[85]

101. In the absence of an instituted lector, other laypersons may be commissioned to proclaim the readings from Sacred Scripture. They should be truly suited to perform this function and should receive careful

---

84   Cf. *Codex Iuris Canonici*, can. 910 § 2; cf. also Interdicasterial Instruction on certain questions regarding the collaboration of the non-ordained faithful in the sacred ministry of priests, *Ecclesiae de mysterio*, 15 August 1997, art. 8: AAS 89 (1997), p. 871.
85   Cf. Sacred Congregation for the Discipline of the Sacraments, Instruction *Immensae caritatis*, 29 January 1973, no. 1: AAS 65 (1973), pp. 265-266; *Codex Iuris Canonici*, can. 230 § 3.

preparation, so that the faithful by listening to the readings from the sacred texts may develop in their hearts a warm and living love for Sacred Scripture.[86]

102. The psalmist's role is to sing the Psalm or other biblical canticle that comes between the readings. To fulfill this function correctly, it is necessary that the psalmist have the ability for singing and a facility in correct pronunciation and diction.

103. Among the faithful, the *schola cantorum* or choir exercises its own liturgical function, ensuring that the parts proper to it, in keeping with the different types of chants, are properly carried out and fostering the active participation of the faithful through the singing.[87] What is said about the choir also applies, in accordance with the relevant norms, to other musicians, especially the organist.

104. It is fitting that there be a cantor or a choir director to lead and sustain the people's singing. When in fact there is no choir, it is up to the cantor to lead the different chants, with the people taking part.[88]

105. The following also exercise a liturgical function:

    a.   The sacristan, who carefully arranges the liturgical books, the vestments, and other things necessary in the celebration of Mass.

    b.   The commentator, who provides the faithful, when appropriate, with brief explanations and commentaries with the purpose of introducing them to the celebration and preparing them to understand it better. The commentator's remarks must

---

86   Cf. Second Vatican Ecumenical Council, Constitution on the Sacred Liturgy, *Sacrosanctum Concilium*, no. 24.

87   Cf. Sacred Congregation of Rites, Instruction *Musicam sacram*, On music in the Liturgy, 5 March 1967, no. 19: AAS 59 (1967), p. 306.

88   Cf. Sacred Congregation of Rites, Instruction *Musicam sacram*, On music in the Liturgy, 5 March 1967, no. 21: AAS 59 (1967), pp. 306-307.

be meticulously prepared and clear though brief. In performing this function the commentator stands in an appropriate place facing the faithful, but not at the ambo.

c. Those who take up the collection in the church.

d. Those who, in some places, meet the faithful at the church entrance, lead them to appropriate places, and direct processions.

106. It is appropriate, at least in cathedrals and in larger churches, to have some competent minister, that is to say a master of ceremonies, to oversee the proper planning of sacred actions and their being carried out by the sacred ministers and the lay faithful with decorum, order, and devotion.

107. The liturgical duties that are not proper to the priest or the deacon and are listed in nos. 100-106 may also be entrusted by a liturgical blessing or a temporary deputation to suitable lay persons chosen by the pastor or rector of the church.[89] All should observe the norms established by the Bishop for his diocese regarding the office of those who serve the priest at the altar.

IV. THE DISTRIBUTION OF DUTIES AND THE PREPARATION OF THE CELEBRATION

108. One and the same priest celebrant must always exercise the presidential office in all of its parts, except for those parts which are proper to a Mass at which the Bishop is present (cf. no. 92).

109. If there are several persons present who are able to exercise the same ministry, nothing forbids their distributing among themselves and performing different parts of the same ministry or duty. For example, one deacon may be assigned to take the sung parts, another to serve at

---

89   Cf. Pontifical Commission for interpreting legal texts, response to *dubium* regarding can. 230 § 2: AAS 86 (1994), p. 541.

the altar; if there are several readings, it is well to distribute them among a number of lectors. The same applies for the other ministries. But it is not at all appropriate that several persons divide a single element of the celebration among themselves, e.g., that the same reading be proclaimed by two lectors, one after the other, except as far as the Passion of the Lord is concerned.

110. If only one minister is present at a Mass with a congregation, that minister may exercise several different duties.

111. Among all who are involved with regard to the rites, pastoral aspects, and music there should be harmony and diligence in the effective preparation of each liturgical celebration in accord with the Missal and other liturgical books. This should take place under the direction of the rector of the church and after the consultation with the faithful about things that directly pertain to them. The priest who presides at the celebration, however, always retains the right of arranging those things that are his own responsibility.[90]

---

90   Cf. Second Vatican Ecumenical Council, Constitution on the Sacred Liturgy, *Sacrosanctum Concilium*, no. 22.

CHAPTER IV
The Different Forms of Celebrating Mass

112. In the local Church, first place should certainly be given, because of its significance, to the Mass at which the Bishop presides, surrounded by his presbyterate, deacons, and lay ministers,[91] and in which the holy people of God participate fully and actively, for it is there that the preeminent expression of the Church is found.

At a Mass celebrated by the Bishop or at which he presides without celebrating the Eucharist, the norms found in the *Caeremoniale Episcoporum* should be observed.[92]

113. Great importance should also be attached to a Mass celebrated with any community, but especially with the parish community, inasmuch as it represents the universal Church gathered at a given time and place. This is particularly true in the communal Sunday celebration.[93]

114. Among those Masses celebrated by some communities, moreover, the conventual Mass, which is a part of the daily Office, or the community Mass, has a particular place. Although such Masses do not have a special form of celebration, it is nevertheless most proper that

---

91   Cf. Second Vatican Ecumenical Council, Constitution on the Sacred Liturgy, *Sacrosanctum Concilium*, no. 41.
92   Cf. *Caeremoniale Episcoporum, editio typica*, 1984, nos. 119-186.
93   Cf. Second Vatican Ecumenical Council, Constitution on the Sacred Liturgy, *Sacrosanctum Concilium*, no. 42; Dogmatic Constitution on the Church, *Lumen gentium*, no. 28; Decree on the Ministry and Life of Priests, *Presbyterorum ordinis*, no. 5; Sacred Congregation of Rites, Instruction *Eucharisticum mysterium*, On the worship of the Eucharist, 25 May 1967, no. 26: AAS 59 (1967), p. 555.

they be celebrated with singing, especially with the full participation of all members of the community, whether of religious or of canons. In these Masses, therefore, individuals should exercise the office proper to the Order or ministry they have received. It is appropriate, therefore, that all the priests who are not bound to celebrate individually for the pastoral benefit of the faithful concelebrate at the conventual or community Mass in so far as it is possible. In addition, all priests belonging to the community who are obliged, as a matter of duty, to celebrate individually for the pastoral benefit of the faithful may also on the same day concelebrate at the conventual or community Mass.[94] For it is preferable that priests who are present at a Eucharistic Celebration, unless excused for a good reason, should as a rule exercise the office proper to their Order and hence take part as concelebrants, wearing the sacred vestments. Otherwise, they wear their proper choir dress or a surplice over a cassock.

I. MASS WITH A CONGREGATION

115. By "Mass with a congregation" is meant a Mass celebrated with the participation of the faithful. It is moreover appropriate, whenever possible, and especially on Sundays and holy days of obligation, that the celebration of this Mass take place with singing and with a suitable number of ministers.[95] It may, however, also be celebrated without singing and with only one minister.

116. If a deacon is present at any celebration of Mass, he should exercise his office. Furthermore, it is desirable that, as a rule, an acolyte, a lector, and a cantor should be there to assist the priest celebrant. In fact, the rite to be described below foresees a greater number of ministers.

---

94   Cf. Sacred Congregation of Rites, Instruction *Eucharisticum mysterium*, On the worship of the Eucharist, 25 May 1967, no. 47: AAS 59 (1967), p. 565.

95   Cf. Sacred Congregation of Rites, Instruction *Eucharisticum mysterium*, On the worship of the Eucharist, 25 May 1967, no. 26: AAS 59 (1967), p. 555; Sacred Congregation of Rites, Instruction *Musicam sacram*, On music in the Liturgy, 5 March 1967, nos. 16, 27: AAS 59 (1967), pp. 305, 308.

The Articles to Be Prepared
117. The altar is to be covered with at least one white cloth. In addition, on or next to the altar are to be placed candlesticks with lighted candles: at least two in any celebration, or even four or six, especially for a Sunday Mass or a holy day of obligation. If the diocesan Bishop celebrates, then seven candles should be used. Also on or close to the altar, there is to be a cross with a figure of Christ crucified. The candles and the cross adorned with a figure of Christ crucified may also be carried in the Entrance Procession. On the altar itself may be placed the *Book of the Gospels*, distinct from the book of other readings, unless it is carried in the Entrance Procession.

118. The following are also to be prepared:

   a. Next to the priest's chair: the Missal and, as needed, a hymnal;
   b. At the ambo: the Lectionary;
   c. On the credence table: the chalice, a corporal, a purificator, and, if appropriate, the pall; the paten and, if needed, ciboria; bread for the Communion of the priest who presides, the deacon, the ministers, and the people; cruets containing the wine and the water, unless all of these are presented by the faithful in procession at the Offertory; the vessel of water to be blessed, if the *asperges* occurs; the Communion-plate for the Communion of the faithful; and whatever is needed for the washing of hands.

It is a praiseworthy practice to cover the chalice with a veil, which may be either the color of the day or white.

119. In the sacristy, the sacred vestments (cf. nos. 337-341) for the priest, the deacon, and other ministers are to be prepared according to the various forms of celebration:

a. For the priest: the alb, the stole, and the chasuble;
b. For the deacon: the alb, the stole, and the dalmatic; the dalmatic may be omitted, however, either out of necessity or on account of a lesser degree of solemnity;
c. For the other ministers: albs or other lawfully approved attire.[96]

All who wear an alb should use a cincture and an amice unless, due to the form of the alb, they are not needed.

When there is an Entrance Procession, the following are also to be prepared: the *Book of the Gospels*; on Sundays and festive days, the thurible and the boat with incense, if incense is used; the cross to be carried in procession; and candlesticks with lighted candles.

A. Mass Without a Deacon
The Introductory Rites
120. Once the people have gathered, the priest and ministers, clad in the sacred vestments, go in procession to the altar in this order:

a. The thurifer carrying a thurible with burning incense, if incense is used;
b. The ministers who carry lighted candles, and between them an acolyte or other minister with the cross;
c. The acolytes and the other ministers;
d. A lector, who may carry the *Book of the Gospels* (though not the Lectionary), which should be slightly elevated;
e. The priest who is to celebrate the Mass.

If incense is used, before the procession begins, the priest puts some in the thurible and blesses it with the Sign of the Cross without saying anything.

---

96   Cf. Interdicasterial Instruction on certain questions regarding the collaboration of the non-ordained faithful in the sacred ministry of priests, *Ecclesiae de mysterio*, 15 August 1997, art. 6: AAS 89 (1997), p. 869.

121. During the procession to the altar, the Entrance chant takes place (cf. nos. 47-48).

122. On reaching the altar, the priest and ministers make a profound bow.

The cross adorned with a figure of Christ crucified and perhaps carried in procession may be placed next to the altar to serve as the altar cross, in which case it ought to be the only cross used; otherwise it is put away in a dignified place. In addition, the candlesticks are placed on the altar or near it. It is a praiseworthy practice that the *Book of the Gospels* be placed upon the altar.

123. The priest goes up to the altar and venerates it with a kiss. Then, as the occasion suggests, he incenses the cross and the altar, walking around the latter.

124. After doing these things, the priest goes to the chair. Once the Entrance chant is concluded, the priest and faithful, all standing, make the Sign of the Cross. The priest says, *In nomine Patris et Filii et Spiritus Sancti* (*In the name of the Father, and of the Son, and of the Holy Spirit*). The people answer, *Amen.*

Then, facing the people and extending his hands, the priest greets the people, using one of the formulas indicated. The priest himself or some other minister may also very briefly introduce the faithful to the Mass of the day.

125. The Act of Penitence follows. Afterwards, the *Kyrie* is sung or said, in keeping with the rubrics (cf. no. 52).

126. For celebrations where it is prescribed, the *Gloria* is either sung or said (cf. no. 53).

127. The priest then invites the people to pray, saying, with hands joined, *Oremus* (*Let us pray*). All pray silently with the priest for a brief time. Then the priest, with hands extended, says the collect, at the end of which the people make the acclamation, *Amen.*

The Liturgy of the Word

128. After the collect, all sit. The priest may, very briefly, introduce the faithful to the Liturgy of the Word. Then the lector goes to the ambo and, from the Lectionary already placed there before Mass, proclaims the first reading, to which all listen. At the end, the lector says the acclamation, *Verbum Domini* (*The word of the Lord*), and all respond, *Deo gratias* (*Thanks be to God*).

Then, as appropriate, a few moments of silence may be observed so that all may meditate on what they have heard.

129. Then the psalmist or even a lector proclaims the verses of the Psalm and the people sing or say the response as usual.

130. If there is to be a second reading before the Gospel, the lector proclaims it from the ambo. All listen and at the end respond to the acclamation, as noted above (no. 128). Then, as appropriate, a few moments of silence may be observed.

131. Afterwards, all rise, and the *Alleluia* or other chant is sung as required by the liturgical season (cf. nos. 62-64).

132. During the singing of the *Alleluia* or other chant, if incense is used, the priest puts some into the thurible and blesses it. Then, with hands joined, he bows profoundly before the altar and quietly says, *Munda cor meum* (*Almighty God, cleanse my heart*).

133. If the *Book of the Gospels* is on the altar, the priest then takes it and goes to the ambo, carrying the *Book of the Gospels* slightly elevated and preceded by the lay ministers, who may carry the thurible

and the candles. Those present turn towards the ambo as a sign of special reverence to the Gospel of Christ.

134. At the ambo, the priest opens the book and, with hands joined, says, *Dominus vobiscum* (*The Lord be with you*), and the people respond, *Et cum spiritu tuo* (*And also with you*). Then he says, *Lectio sancti Evangelii* (*A reading from the holy Gospel*), making the sign of the cross with his thumb on the book and on his forehead, mouth, and breast, which everyone else does as well. The people say the acclamation, *Gloria tibi, Domine* (*Glory to you, Lord*). The priest incenses the book, if incense is used (cf. nos. 276-277). Then he proclaims the Gospel and at the end says the acclamation, *Verbum Domini* (*The Gospel of the Lord*), to which all respond, *Laus tibi, Christe* (*Praise to you, Lord Jesus Christ*). The priest kisses the book, saying quietly, *Per evangelica dicta* (*May the words of the Gospel*).

135. If no lector is present, the priest himself proclaims all the readings and the Psalm, standing at the ambo. If incense is used, remaining at the ambo he puts some into the thurible, blesses it, and, bowing profoundly, says, *Munda cor meum* (*Almighty God, cleanse my heart*).

136. The priest, standing at the chair or at the ambo itself or, when appropriate, in another suitable place, gives the homily. When the homily is completed, a period of silence may be observed.

137. The Creed is sung or recited by the priest together with the people (cf. no. 68) with everyone standing. At the words *et incarnatus est* (*by the power of the Holy Spirit . . . and became man*) all make a profound bow; but on the solemnities of the Annunciation and of the Nativity of the Lord, all genuflect.

138. After the recitation of the Creed, the priest, standing at the chair with hands joined, by means of a brief introduction invites the faithful to participate in the Prayer of the Faithful. Then the cantor, the lector, or another person announces the intentions from the ambo or from

some other suitable place while facing the people, who take their part by responding in supplication. After the intentions, the priest, with hands extended, concludes the petitions with a prayer.

The Liturgy of the Eucharist
139. When the Prayer of the Faithful is completed, all sit, and the Offertory chant begins (cf. no. 74).

An acolyte or other lay minister arranges the corporal, the purificator, the chalice, the pall, and the Missal upon the altar.

140. It is appropriate for the faithful's participation to be expressed by an offering, whether of the bread and wine for the celebration of the Eucharist or of other gifts for the relief of the needs of the Church and of the poor.

The offerings of the faithful are received by the priest, assisted by the acolyte or other minister. The bread and wine for the Eucharist are carried to the celebrant, who places them upon the altar, while other gifts are put in another appropriate place (cf. no. 73).

141. At the altar the priest accepts the paten with the bread. With both hands he holds it slightly raised above the altar and says quietly, *Benedictus es, Domine* (*Blessed are you, Lord*). Then he places the paten with the bread on the corporal.

142. After this, as the minister presents the cruets, the priest stands at the side of the altar and pours wine and a little water into the chalice, saying quietly, *Per huius aquae* (*By the mystery of this water*). He returns to the middle of the altar, takes the chalice with both hands, raises it a little, and says quietly, *Benedictus es, Domine* (*Blessed are you, Lord*). Then he places the chalice on the corporal and covers it with a pall, as appropriate.

If, however, there is no Offertory chant and the organ is not played, in the presentation of the bread and wine the priest may say the formulas of blessing aloud, to which the people make the acclamation, *Benedictus Deus in saecula* (*Blessed be God for ever*).

143. After placing the chalice upon the altar, the priest bows profoundly and says quietly, *In spiritu humilitatis* (*Lord God, we ask you to receive us*).

144. If incense is used, the priest then puts some in the thurible, blesses it without saying anything, and incenses the offerings, the cross, and the altar. A minister, while standing at the side of the altar, incenses the priest and then the people.

145. After the prayer *In spiritu humilitatis* (*Lord God, we ask you to receive us*) or after the incensation, the priest washes his hands standing at the side of the altar and, as the minister pours the water, says quietly, *Lava me, Domine* (*Lord, wash away my iniquity*).

146. Upon returning to the middle of the altar, the priest, facing the people and extending and then joining his hands, invites the people to pray, saying, *Orate, fratres* (*Pray, brethren*). The people rise and make their response: *Suscipiat Dominus* (*May the Lord accept*). Then the priest, with hands extended, says the prayer over the offerings. At the end the people make the acclamation, *Amen*.

147. Then the priest begins the Eucharistic Prayer. In accordance with the rubrics (cf. no. 365), he selects a Eucharistic Prayer from those found in the *Roman Missal* or approved by the Apostolic See. The Eucharistic Prayer demands, by its very nature, that only the priest say it in virtue of his ordination. The people, for their part, should associate themselves with the priest in faith and in silence, as well as through their parts as prescribed in the course of the Eucharistic Prayer: namely, the responses in the Preface dialogue, the *Sanctus*, the acclamation after the consecration, the acclamatory *Amen* after the final doxology, as well as other acclamations approved by the Conference of Bishops and recognized by the Holy See.

It is very appropriate that the priest sing those parts of the Eucharistic Prayer for which musical notation is provided.

148. As he begins the Eucharistic Prayer, the priest extends his hands and sings or says, *Dominus vobiscum* (*The Lord be with you*). The people respond, *Et cum spiritu tuo* (*And also with you*). As he continues, *Sursum corda* (*Lift up your hearts*), he raises his hands. The people respond, *Habemus ad Dominum* (*We lift them up to the Lord*). Then the priest, with hands outstretched, adds, *Gratias agamus Domino Deo nostro* (*Let us give thanks to the Lord, our God*), and the people respond, *Dignum et iustum est* (*It is right to give him thanks and praise*). Next, the priest, with hands extended, continues the Preface. At its conclusion, he joins his hands and, together with everyone present, sings or says aloud the *Sanctus* (cf. no. 79b).

149. The priest continues the Eucharistic Prayer in accordance with the rubrics that are set forth in each of the Prayers.

If the celebrant is a Bishop, in the Prayers, after the words *Papa nostro N.* (*N., our Pope*), he adds, *et me, indigno famulo tuo* (*and me, your unworthy servant*). If, however, the Bishop is celebrating outside his own diocese, after the words *Papa nostro N.* (*N., our Pope*), he adds, *et me indigno famulo tuo, et fratre meo N., Episcopo huius Ecclesiae N.* (*me, your unworthy servant, and my brother N., the Bishop of this Church of N.*).

The diocesan Bishop or anyone equivalent to him in law must be mentioned by means of this formula: *una cum famulo tuo Papa nostro N. et Episcopo* (or *Vicario, Prelato, Praefecto, Abbate*) (*together with your servant N., our Pope, and N., our Bishop* [or *Vicar, Prelate, Prefect, Abbot*]).

It is permitted to mention Coadjutor and Auxiliary Bishops in the Eucharistic Prayer, but not other Bishops who happen to be present.

When several are to be named, this is done with the collective formula *et Episcopo nostro N. eiusque Episcopis adiutoribus* (*N., our Bishop and his assistant Bishops*).

In each of the Eucharistic Prayers, these formulas are to be modified according to the requirements of grammar.

150. A little before the consecration, when appropriate, a server rings a bell as a signal to the faithful. According to local custom, the server also rings the bell as the priest shows the host and then the chalice.

If incense is used, a server incenses the host and the chalice when each is shown to the people after the consecration.

151. After the consecration when the priest has said, *Mysterium fidei* (*Let us proclaim the mystery of faith*), the people sing or say an acclamation using one of the prescribed formulas.

At the end of the Eucharistic Prayer, the priest takes the paten with the host and the chalice and elevates them both while alone singing or saying the doxology, *Per ipsum* (*Through him*). At the end the people make the acclamation, *Amen.* Then the priest places the paten and the chalice on the corporal.

152. After the Eucharistic Prayer is concluded, the priest, with hands joined, says the introduction to the Lord's Prayer. With hands extended, he then says this prayer together with the people.

153. After the Lord's Prayer is concluded, the priest alone, with hands extended, says the embolism *Libera nos* (*Deliver us*). At the end, the people make the acclamation, *Quia tuum est regnum* (*For the kingdom*).

154. Then the priest, with hands extended, says aloud the prayer, *Domine Iesu Christe, qui dixisti* (*Lord Jesus Christ, you said*). After

this prayer is concluded, extending and then joining his hands, he gives the greeting of peace while facing the people and saying, *Pax Domini sit simper vobiscum* (*The peace of the Lord be with you always*). The people answer, *Et cum spiritu tuo* (*And also with you*). Afterwards, when appropriate, the priest adds, *Offerte vobis pacem* (*Let us offer each other the sign of peace*).

The priest may give the sign of peace to the ministers but always remains within the sanctuary, so as not to disturb the celebration. In the dioceses of the United States of America, for a good reason, on special occasions (for example, in the case of a funeral, a wedding, or when civic leaders are present) the priest may offer the sign of peace to a few of the faithful near the sanctuary. At the same time, in accord with the decisions of the Conference of Bishops, all offer one another a sign that expresses peace, communion, and charity. While the sign of peace is being given, one may say, *Pax Domini sit semper tecum* (*The peace of the Lord be with you always*), to which the response is *Amen*.

155. The priest then takes the host and breaks it over the paten. He places a small piece in the chalice, saying quietly, *Haec commixtio* (*May this mingling*). Meanwhile the *Agnus Dei* is sung or said by the choir and congregation (cf. no. 83).

156. Then the priest, with hands joined, quietly says the preparatory prayer of Communion: *Domine Iesu Christe, Fili Dei vivi* (*Lord Jesus Christ, Son of the living God*) or *Perceptio Corporis et Sanguinis* (*Lord Jesus Christ, with faith in your love and mercy*).

157. When the prayer is concluded, the priest genuflects, takes the host consecrated in the same Mass, and, holding it slightly raised above the paten or above the chalice, while facing the people, says, *Ecce Agnus Dei* (*This is the Lamb of God*). With the people he adds, *Domine, non sum dignus* (*Lord, I am not worthy*).

158. After this, standing and turned toward the altar, the priest says quietly, *Corpus Christi custodiat me in vitam aeternam* (*May the Body of Christ bring me to everlasting life*) and reverently receives the Body of Christ. Then he takes the chalice, saying quietly, *Sanguis Christi custodiat me in vitam aeternam* (*May the Blood of Christ bring me to everlasting life*), and reverently receives the Blood of Christ.

159. The Communion chant begins while the priest is receiving the Sacrament (cf. no. 86).

160. The priest then takes the paten or ciborium and goes to the communicants, who, as a rule, approach in a procession.

The faithful are not permitted to take the consecrated bread or the sacred chalice by themselves and, still less, to hand them from one to another. The norm for reception of Holy Communion in the dioceses of the United States is standing. Communicants should not be denied Holy Communion because they kneel. Rather, such instances should be addressed pastorally, by providing the faithful with proper catechesis on the reasons for this norm.

When receiving Holy Communion, the communicant bows his or her head before the Sacrament as a gesture of reverence and receives the Body of the Lord from the minister. The consecrated host may be received either on the tongue or in the hand, at the discretion of each communicant. When Holy Communion is received under both kinds, the sign of reverence is also made before receiving the Precious Blood.

161. If Communion is given only under the species of bread, the priest raises the host slightly and shows it to each, saying, *Corpus Christi* (*The Body of Christ*). The communicant replies, *Amen*, and receives the Sacrament either on the tongue or, where this is allowed and if the communicant so chooses, in the hand. As soon as the communicant receives the host, he or she consumes it entirely.

If, however, Communion is given under both kinds, the rite prescribed in nos. 284-287 is followed.

162. The priest may be assisted in the distribution of Communion by other priests who happen to be present. If such priests are not present and there is a very large number of communicants, the priest may call upon extraordinary ministers to assist him, i.e., duly instituted acolytes or even other faithful who have been deputed for this purpose.[97] In case of necessity, the priest may depute suitable faithful for this single occasion.[98]

These ministers should not approach the altar before the priest has received Communion, and they are always to receive from the hands of the priest celebrant the vessel containing either species of the Most Holy Eucharist for distribution to the faithful.

163. When the distribution of Communion is finished, the priest himself immediately and completely consumes at the altar any consecrated wine that happens to remain; as for any consecrated hosts that are left, he either consumes them at the altar or carries them to the place designated for the reservation of the Eucharist.

Upon returning to the altar, the priest collects any fragments that may remain. Then, standing at the altar or at the credence table, he purifies the paten or ciborium over the chalice, then purifies the chalice, saying quietly, *Quod ore sumpsimus* (*Lord, may I receive*), and dries the chalice with a purificator. If the vessels are purified at the altar, they are carried to the credence table by a minister. Nevertheless, it is also permitted, especially if there are several vessels to be purified, to leave them suitably

---

97   Cf. Sacred Congregation for the Sacraments and Divine Worship, Instruction *Inaestimabile donum*, 3 April 1980, no. 10: AAS 72 (1980), p. 336; Interdicasterial Instruction on certain questions regarding the collaboration of the non-ordained faithful in the sacred ministry of priests, *Ecclesiae de mysterio*, 15 August 1997, art. 8: AAS 89 (1997), p. 871.

98   Cf. below, Appendix, Order of Commissioning a Minister to Distribute Holy Communion on a Single Occasion, p. 1253.

covered on a corporal, either at the altar or at the credence table, and to purify them immediately after Mass following the dismissal of the people.

164. Afterwards, the priest may return to the chair. A sacred silence may now be observed for some period of time, or a Psalm or another canticle of praise or a hymn may be sung (cf. no. 88).

165. Then, standing at the chair or at the altar and facing the people the priest, with hands joined says, *Oremus* (*Let us pray*); then, with hands extended, he recites the prayer after Communion. A brief period of silence may precede the prayer, unless this has been already observed immediately after Communion. At the end of the prayer the people say the acclamation, *Amen*.

The Concluding Rites
166. When the prayer after Communion is concluded, brief announcements to the people may be made, if they are needed.

167. Then the priest, extending his hands, greets the people, saying, *Dominus vobiscum* (*The Lord be with you*). They answer, *Et cum spiritu tuo* (*And also with you*). The priest, joining his hands again and then immediately placing his left hand on his breast, raises his right hand and adds, *Benedicat vos omnipotens Deus* (*May Almighty God bless you*) and, as he makes the Sign of the Cross over the people, continues, *Pater, et Filius, et Spiritus Sanctus* (*the Father, and the Son, and the Holy Spirit*). All answer, *Amen*.

On certain days and occasions this blessing, in accordance with the rubrics, is expanded and expressed by a prayer over the People or another more solemn formula.

A Bishop blesses the people with the appropriate formula, making the Sign of the Cross three times over the people.[99]

---

99   Cf. *Caeremoniale Episcoporum, editio typica*, 1984, nos. 1118-1121.

168. Immediately after the blessing, with hands joined, the priest adds, *Ite, missa est* (*The Mass is ended, go in peace*), and all answer, *Deo gratias* (*Thanks be to God*).

169. Then, as a rule, the priest venerates the altar with a kiss and, after making a profound bow with the lay ministers, departs with them.

170. If, however, another liturgical action follows the Mass, the concluding rites, that is, the greeting, the blessing, and the dismissal, are omitted.

B. Mass with a Deacon

171. When he is present at the Eucharistic Celebration, a deacon should exercise his ministry, wearing sacred vestments. For the deacon

    a.   Assists the priest and remains at his side;

    b.   Ministers at the altar, with the chalice as well as the book;

    c.   Proclaims the Gospel and, at the direction of the priest celebrant, may preach the homily (cf. no. 66);

    d.   Guides the faithful by appropriate introductions and explanations, and announces the intentions of the Prayer of the Faithful;

    e.   Assists the priest celebrant in distributing Communion, and purifies and arranges the sacred vessels;

    f.   As needed, fulfills the duties of other ministers himself if none of them is present.

The Introductory Rites

172. Carrying the *Book of the Gospels* slightly elevated, the deacon precedes the priest as he approaches the altar or else walks at the priest's side.

173. When he reaches the altar, if he is carrying the *Book of the Gospels*, he omits the sign of reverence and goes up to the altar. It is particularly appropriate that he should place the *Book of the Gospels* on the altar, after which, together with the priest, he venerates the altar with a kiss.

If, however, he is not carrying the *Book of the Gospels*, he makes a profound bow to the altar with the priest in the customary way and with him venerates the altar with a kiss.

Lastly, if incense is used, he assists the priest in putting some into the thurible and in incensing the cross and the altar.

174. After the incensation of the altar, he goes to the chair together with the priest, takes his place there at the side of the priest and assists him as necessary.

The Liturgy of the Word
175. If incense is used, the deacon assists the priest when he puts incense in the thurible during the singing of the *Alleluia* or other chant. Then he makes a profound bow before the priest and asks for the blessing, saying in a low voice, *Iube, domine, benedicere* (*Father, give me your blessing*). The priest blesses him, saying, *Dominus sit in corde tuo* (*The Lord be in your heart*). The deacon signs himself with the Sign of the Cross and responds, *Amen*. Having bowed to the altar, he then takes up the *Book of the Gospels* which was placed upon it. He proceeds to the ambo, carrying the book slightly elevated. He is preceded by a thurifer, carrying a thurible with smoking incense, and by servers with lighted candles. There the deacon, with hands joined, greets the people, saying, *Dominus vobiscum* (*The Lord be with you*). Then, at the words *Lectio sancti Evangelii* (*A reading from the holy Gospel*), he signs the book with his thumb and, afterwards, himself on his forehead, mouth, and breast. He incenses the book and proclaims the Gospel reading. When the reading is concluded, he says the acclamation *Verbum Domini* (*The Gospel of the Lord*), and all respond, *Laus tibi, Christe* (*Praise to you, Lord Jesus Christ*). He then venerates the book with a kiss, saying privately, *Per evangelica dicta* (*May the words of the Gospel*), and returns to the priest's side.

When the deacon is assisting the Bishop, he carries the book to him to be kissed, or else kisses it himself, saying quietly, *Per evangelica dicta dicta* (*May the words of the Gospel*). In more solemn celebrations, as the occasion suggests, a Bishop may impart a blessing to the people with the *Book of the Gospels.*

Lastly, the deacon may carry the *Book of the Gospels* to the credence table or to another appropriate and dignified place.

176. If, in addition, there is no other suitable lector present, the deacon should proclaim the other readings as well.

177. After the introduction by the priest it is the deacon himself who normally announces the intentions of the Prayer of the Faithful, from the ambo.

The Liturgy of the Eucharist
178. After the Prayer of the Faithful, while the priest remains at the chair, the deacon prepares the altar, assisted by the acolyte, but it is the deacon's place to take care of the sacred vessels himself. He also assists the priest in receiving the people's gifts. Next, he hands the priest the paten with the bread to be consecrated, pours wine and a little water into the chalice, saying quietly, *Per huius aquae (By the mystery of this water)*, and after this presents the chalice to the priest. He may also carry out the preparation of the chalice at the credence table. If incense is used, the deacon assists the priest during the incensation of the gifts, the cross, and the altar; afterwards, the deacon himself or the acolyte incenses the priest and the people.

179. During the Eucharistic Prayer, the deacon stands near the priest but slightly behind him, so that when needed he may assist the priest with the chalice or the Missal.

From the epiclesis until the priest shows the chalice, the deacon normally remains kneeling. If several deacons are present, one of them may place incense in the thurible for the consecration and incense the host and the chalice as they are shown to the people.

180. At the final doxology of the Eucharistic Prayer, the deacon stands next to the priest, holding the chalice elevated while the priest elevates the paten with the host, until the people have responded with the acclamation, *Amen*.

181. After the priest has said the prayer at the Rite of Peace and the greeting *Pax Domini sit semper vobiscum* (*The peace of the Lord be with you always*) and the people have responded, *Et cum spiritu tuo* (*And also with you*), the deacon, if it is appropriate, invites all to exchange the sign of peace. He faces the people and, with hands joined, says, *Offerte vobis pacem* (*Let us offer each other the sign of peace*). Then he himself receives the sign of peace from the priest and may offer it to those other ministers who are closer to him.

182. After the priest's Communion, the deacon receives Communion under both kinds from the priest himself and then assists the priest in distributing Communion to the people. If Communion is given under both kinds, the deacon himself administers the chalice to the communicants; and, when the distribution is completed, he immediately and reverently consumes at the altar all of the Blood of Christ that remains, assisted if necessary by other deacons and priests.

183. When the distribution of Communion is completed, the deacon returns to the altar with the priest and collects the fragments, if any remain, and then carries the chalice and other sacred vessels to the credence table, where he purifies them and arranges them in the usual way while the priest returns to the chair. It is also permissible to leave the vessels that need to be purified, suitably covered, at the credence table on a corporal, and to purify them immediately after Mass following the dismissal of the people.

The Concluding Rites

184. Once the prayer after Communion has been said, the deacon makes brief announcements to the people, if indeed any need to be made, unless the priest prefers to do this himself.

185. If a prayer over the people or a solemn formula for the blessing is used, the deacon says, *Inclinate vos ad benedictionem* (*Bow your heads and pray for God's blessing*). After the priest's blessing, the deacon, with hands joined and facing the people, dismisses them, saying, *Ite, missa est* (*The Mass is ended, go in peace*).

186. Then, together with the priest, the deacon venerates the altar with a kiss, makes a profound bow, and departs in a manner similar to the procession beforehand.

C. The Duties of the Acolyte
187. The duties that the acolyte may carry out are of various kinds and several may coincide. Hence, it is desirable that these duties be suitably distributed among several acolytes. If, however, only one acolyte is present, he should perform the more important duties while the rest are to be distributed among several ministers.

The Introductory Rites
188. In the procession to the altar, the acolyte may carry the cross, walking between two ministers with lighted candles. Upon reaching the altar, the acolyte places the cross upright near the altar so that it may serve as the altar cross; otherwise, he puts it in a worthy place. Then he takes his place in the sanctuary.

189. Through the entire celebration, the acolyte is to approach the priest or the deacon, whenever necessary, in order to present the book to them and to assist them in any other way required. Thus it is appropriate, insofar as possible, that the acolyte occupy a place from which he can conveniently carry out his ministry either at the chair or at the altar.

The Liturgy of the Eucharist
190. If no deacon is present, after the Prayer of the Faithful is concluded and while the priest remains at the chair, the acolyte places the corporal, the purificator, the chalice, the pall, and the Missal on the altar. Then, if necessary, the acolyte assists the priest in receiving the gifts of

the people and, if appropriate, brings the bread and wine to the altar and hands them to the priest. If incense is used, the acolyte presents the thurible to the priest and assists him while he incenses the gifts, the cross, and the altar. Then the acolyte incenses the priest and the people.

191. A duly instituted acolyte, as an extraordinary minister, may, if necessary, assist the priest in giving Communion to the people.[100] If Communion is given under both kinds, when no deacon is present, the acolyte administers the chalice to the communicants or holds the chalice if Communion is given by intinction.

192. Likewise, when the distribution of Communion is completed, a duly instituted acolyte helps the priest or deacon to purify and arrange the sacred vessels. When no deacon is present, a duly instituted acolyte carries the sacred vessels to the credence table and there purifies, wipes, and arranges them in the usual way.

193. After the celebration of Mass, the acolyte and other ministers return in procession to the sacristy, together with the deacon and the priest in the same way and order in which they entered.

D. The Duties of the Lector
Introductory Rites
194. In coming to the altar, when no deacon is present, the lector, wearing approved attire, may carry the *Book of the Gospels*, which is to be slightly elevated. In that case, the lector walks in front of the priest but otherwise along with the other ministers.

195. Upon reaching the altar, the lector makes a profound bow with the others. If he is carrying the *Book of the Gospels*, he approaches the

---

100   Cf. Paul VI, Apostolic Letter *Ministeria quaedam*, 15 August 1972: AAS 64 (1972), p. 532.

altar and places the *Book of the Gospels* upon it. Then the lector takes his own place in the sanctuary with the other ministers.

The Liturgy of the Word
196. The lector reads from the ambo the readings that precede the Gospel. If there is no psalmist, the lector may also proclaim the responsorial Psalm after the first reading.

197. When no deacon is present, the lector, after the introduction by the priest, may announce from the ambo the intentions of the Prayer of the Faithful.

198. If there is no singing at the Entrance or at Communion and the antiphons in the Missal are not recited by the faithful, the lector may read them at the appropriate time (cf. nos. 48, 87).

II. CONCELEBRATED MASS
199. Concelebration, which appropriately expresses the unity of the priesthood, of the Sacrifice, and also of the whole People of God, is prescribed by the rite itself for the Ordination of a Bishop and of priests, at the blessing of an abbot, and at the Chrism Mass.

Unless the good of the Christian faithful requires or suggests otherwise, concelebration is also recommended at

a. The Evening Mass of the Lord's Supper;
b. The Mass during Councils, meetings of Bishops, and synods;
c. The conventual Mass and the principal Mass in churches and oratories;
d. Masses at any kind of meeting of priests, either secular or religious.[101]

---

101   Cf. Second Vatican Ecumenical Council, Constitution on the Sacred Liturgy, *Sacrosanctum Concilium*, no. 57; *Codex Iuris Canonici*, can. 902.

An individual priest is, however, permitted to celebrate the Eucharist individually, though not at the same time as a concelebration is taking place in the same church or oratory. On Holy Thursday, however, and for Mass of the Easter Vigil, it is not permitted to celebrate individually.

200. Visiting priests should be gladly welcomed to Eucharistic concelebration, as long as their priestly standing is ascertained.

201. Where there is a large number of priests, concelebration may take place even several times on the same day, wherever necessity or pastoral benefit suggest it. Nevertheless, it must be held at different times or in distinct sacred places.[102]

202. It is for the Bishop, in accordance with the norm of law, to regulate the discipline for concelebration in all churches and oratories of his diocese.

203. To be held in high regard is that concelebration in which the priests of each diocese concelebrate with their own Bishop at a stational Mass, especially on the more solemn days of the liturgical year, at the Ordination Mass of a new Bishop of the diocese or of his Coadjutor or Auxiliary, at the Chrism Mass, at the Evening Mass of the Lord's Supper, at celebrations of the Founder Saint of a local Church or the Patron of the diocese, on anniversaries of the Bishop, and, lastly, on the occasion of a Synod or a pastoral visitation.

For this same reason, concelebration is recommended whenever priests gather together with their own Bishop either on the occasion of a retreat or at any other meeting. In these instances the sign of the unity of the priesthood and also of the Church inherent in every concelebration is made more clearly manifest.[103]

---

102   Cf. Sacred Congregation of Rites, Instruction *Eucharisticum mysterium*, On the worship of the Eucharist, 25 May 1967, no. 47: AAS 59 (1967), p. 566.

103   Cf. Sacred Congregation of Rites, Instruction *Eucharisticum mysterium*, On the worship of the Eucharist, 25 May 1967, no. 47: AAS 59 (1967), p. 565.

204. For a particular reason, having to do either with the significance of the rite or of the festivity, the faculty is given to celebrate or concelebrate more than once on the same day in the following cases:

    a. A priest who has celebrated or concelebrated the Chrism Mass on Holy Thursday may also celebrate or concelebrate the Evening Mass of the Lord's Supper;

    b. A priest who has celebrated or concelebrated the Mass of the Easter Vigil may celebrate or concelebrate Mass during the day on Easter Sunday;

    c. On the Nativity of the Lord (Christmas Day), all priests may celebrate or concelebrate three Masses, provided the Masses are celebrated at their proper times of day;

    d. On the Commemoration of All the Faithful Departed (All Souls' Day), all priests may celebrate or concelebrate three Masses, provided that the celebrations take place at different times, and that the norms established regarding the application of second and third Masses are observed;[104]

    e. A priest who concelebrates with the Bishop or his delegate at a Synod or pastoral visitation, or concelebrates on the occasion of a meeting of priests, may celebrate Mass again for the benefit of the faithful. This holds also, with due regard for the prescriptions of law, for groups of religious.

205. A concelebrated Mass, whatever its form, is arranged in accordance with the norms commonly in force (cf. nos. 112-198), except for those matters that are to be observed, even with appropriate adaptation to circumstances, as set forth below.

206. No one is ever to enter into a concelebration or to be admitted as a concelebrant once the Mass has already begun.

---

104   Cf. Benedict XV, Apostolic Constitution *Incruentum altaris sacrificium*, 10 August 1915: AAS 7 (1915), pp. 401-404.

207. In the sanctuary there should be prepared

    a.   Seats and texts for the concelebrating priests;

    b.   On the credence table: a chalice of sufficient size or else several chalices.

208. If a deacon is not present, his proper duties are to be carried out by some of the concelebrants.

In the absence also of other ministers, their proper parts may be entrusted to other suitable members of the faithful; otherwise, they are carried out by some of the concelebrants.

209. In the vesting room or other suitable place, the concelebrants put on the sacred vestments they customarily wear when celebrating Mass individually. Should, however, a good reason arise, (e.g., a large number of concelebrants or a lack of vestments), concelebrants other than the principal celebrant may omit the chasuble and simply wear the stole over the alb.

The Introductory Rites

210. When everything has been properly arranged, the procession moves as usual through the church to the altar, the concelebrating priests walking ahead of the principal celebrant.

211. On reaching the altar, the concelebrants and the principal celebrant, after making a profound bow, venerate the altar with a kiss, then go to their designated seats. The principal celebrant, if appropriate, also incenses the cross and the altar and then goes to the chair.

The Liturgy of the Word

212. During the Liturgy of the Word, the concelebrants remain at their places, sitting or standing whenever the principal celebrant does.

When the *Alleluia* is begun, all rise, except for a Bishop, who puts incense into the thurible without saying anything and blesses the deacon or, if there is no deacon, the concelebrant who is to proclaim the Gospel. In a concelebration where a priest presides, however, the concelebrant who in the absence of a deacon proclaims the Gospel neither requests nor receives the blessing of the principal celebrant.

213. The homily is usually given by the principal celebrant or by one of the concelebrants.

The Liturgy of the Eucharist
214. The Preparation of the Gifts (cf. nos. 139-146) is carried out by the principal celebrant, while the other concelebrants remain at their places.

215. After the prayer over the offerings has been said by the principal celebrant, the concelebrants approach the altar and stand around it, but in such a way that they do not obstruct the execution of the rites and that the sacred action may be seen clearly by the faithful. They should not be in the deacon's way whenever he needs to go to the altar to perform his ministry.

The deacon exercises his ministry at the altar whenever he needs to assist with the chalice and the Missal. However, insofar as possible, he stands back slightly, behind the concelebrating priests standing around the principal celebrant.

The Manner of Speaking the Eucharistic Prayer
216. The Preface is sung or said by the principal priest celebrant alone; but the *Sanctus* is sung or recited by all the concelebrants, together with the congregation and the choir.

217. After the *Sanctus*, the priest concelebrants continue the Eucharistic Prayer in the way described below. Unless otherwise indicated, only the principal celebrant makes the gestures.

218. The parts spoken by all the concelebrants together and especially the words of consecration, which all are bound to say, are to be said in such a way that the concelebrants speak them in a very low voice and that the principal celebrant's voice be clearly heard. In this way the words can be better understood by the people.

It is a praiseworthy practice for the parts that are to be said by all the concelebrants together and for which musical notation is provided in the Missal to be sung.

Eucharistic Prayer I, or The Roman Canon
219. In Eucharistic Prayer I, or the Roman Canon, the prayer *Te igitur* (*We come to you, Father*) is said by the principal celebrant alone, with hands extended.

220. It is appropriate that the commemoration of the living (the *Memento*) and the *Communicantes* (*In union with the whole Church*) be assigned to one or other of the concelebrating priests, who then speaks these prayers aloud, with hands extended.

221. The *Hanc igitur* (*Father, accept this offering*) is likewise said by the principal celebrant alone, with hands extended.

222. From the *Quam oblationem* (*Bless and approve our offering*) up to and including the *Supplices* (*Almighty God, we pray that your angel*), the principal celebrant alone makes the gestures, while all the concelebrants speak everything together, in this manner:

    a. The *Quam oblationem* (*Bless and approve our offering*) with hands extended toward the offerings;

    b. The *Qui pridie* (*The day before he suffered*) and the *Simili modo* (*When supper was ended*) with hands joined;

c. While speaking the words of the Lord, each extends his right hand toward the bread and toward the chalice, if this seems appropriate; as the host and the chalice are shown, however, they look toward them and afterwards bow profoundly;

d. The *Unde et memores* (*Father, we celebrate the memory*) and the *Supra quae* (*Look with favor*) with hands extended;

e. From the *Supplices* (*Almighty God, we pray that your angel*) up to and including the words *ex hac altaris participatione* (*as we receive from this altar*), they bow with hands joined; then they stand upright and cross themselves at the words *omni benedictione et gratia repleamur* (*let us be filled with every grace and blessing*).

223. The commemoration of the dead (*Memento*) and the *Nobis quoque peccatoribus* (*Though we are sinners*) are appropriately assigned to one or other of the concelebrants, who speaks them aloud alone, with hands extended.

224. At the words *Nobis quoque peccatoribus* (*Though we are sinners*) all the concelebrants strike their breast.

225. The *Per quem haec omnia* (*Through him you give us all these gifts*) is said by the principal celebrant alone.

Eucharistic Prayer II
226. In Eucharistic Prayer II the *Vere sanctus* (*Lord, you are holy indeed*) is spoken by the principal celebrant alone, with hands extended.

227. From the *Haec ergo dona* (*Let your Spirit come upon*) to the *Et supplices* (*May all of us who share*) inclusive, all the concelebrants speak all the following together:

a. The *Haec ergo dona* (*Let your Spirit come upon*) with hands extended toward the offerings;

b. The *Qui cum passioni* (*Before he was given up to death*) and the *Simili modo* (*When supper was ended*) with hands joined;

c. While speaking the words of the Lord, each extends his right hand toward the bread and toward the chalice, if this seems appropriate; as the host and the chalice are shown, however, they look toward them and afterwards bow profoundly;

d. The *Memores igitur* (*In memory of his death*) and the *Et supplices* (*May all of us who share*) with hands extended.

228. The intercessions for the living, *Recordare, Domine* (*Lord, remember your Church*), and for the dead, *Memento etiam fratrum nostrorum* (*Remember our brothers and sisters*), are appropriately assigned to one or other of the concelebrants, who speaks them aloud alone, with hands extended.

Eucharistic Prayer III

229. In Eucharistic Prayer III, the *Vere sanctus* (*Father, you are holy indeed*) is spoken by the principal celebrant alone, with hands extended.

230. From the *Supplices ergo te, Domine* (*And so, Father, we bring you these gifts*) to the *Respice, quaesumus* (*Look with favor*) inclusive, all the concelebrants speak all the following together:

a. The *Supplices ergo te, Domine* (*And so, Father, we bring you these gifts*) with hands extended toward the offerings;

b. The *Ipse enim in qua nocte tradebatur* (*On the night he was betrayed*) and the *Simili modo* (*When supper was ended*) with hands joined;

c. While speaking the words of the Lord, each extends his right hand toward the bread and toward the chalice, if this seems appropriate; as the host and the chalice are shown, however, they look at them and, afterwards, bow profoundly;

    d.   The *Memores igitur* (*Father, calling to mind*) and the *Respice, quaesumus* (*Look with favor*) with hands outstretched.

231. The intercessions *Ipse nos* (*May he make us an everlasting gift*), *Haec hostia nostrae reconciliationis* (*Lord, may this sacrifice*), and *Fratres nostros* (*Welcome into your kingdom*) are appropriately assigned to one or other of the concelebrants, who speaks them aloud alone, with hands extended.

Eucharistic Prayer IV

232. In Eucharistic Prayer IV, the *Confitemur tibi, Pater sancte* (*Father, we acknowledge*) up to and including the words *omnem sanctificationem compleret* (*bring us the fullness of grace*) is spoken by the principal celebrant alone, with hands extended.

233. From the *Quaesumus, igitur, Domine* (*Father, may this Holy Spirit*) to the *Respice, Domine* (*Lord, look upon the sacrifice*) inclusive, all the concelebrants speak all the following together:

    a.   The *Quaesumus igitur, Domine* (*Father, may this Holy Spirit*) with hands extended toward the offerings;

    b.   The *Ipse enim, cum hora venisset* (*He always loved those*) and the *Simili modo* (*When supper was ended*) with hands joined;

    c.   While speaking the words of the Lord, each extends his right hand toward the bread and toward the chalice, if this seems appropriate; as the host and the chalice are shown, however, they look toward them and afterwards bow profoundly;

    d.   The *Unde et nos* (*Father, we now celebrate*) and the *Respice, Domine* (*Lord, look upon this sacrifice*) with hands outstretched.

234. The intercessions *Nunc ergo, Domine, omnium recordare* (*Lord, remember those*) and *Nobis omnibus* (*Father, in your mercy*) are appropriately assigned to one or other of the concelebrants, who speaks them aloud alone, with hands extended.

235. As to other Eucharistic Prayers approved by the Apostolic See, the norms established for each one are to be observed.

236. The concluding doxology of the Eucharistic Prayer is spoken solely by the principal priest celebrant and, if this is desired, together with the other concelebrants, but not by the faithful.

The Communion Rite
237. Then the principal celebrant, with hands joined, says the introduction to the Lord's Prayer. Then, with hands extended, he says the prayer itself together with the other concelebrants, who also pray with hands extended and with the people.

238. *Libera nos* (*Deliver us*) is said by the principal celebrant alone, with hands extended. All the concelebrants, together with the people, sing or say the final acclamation *Quia tuum est regnum* (*For the kingdom*).

239. After the deacon or, when no deacon is present, one of the concelebrants has said the invitation *Offerte vobis pacem* (*Let us offer each other the sign of peace*), all exchange the sign of peace with one another. The concelebrants who are nearer the principal celebrant receive the sign of peace from him before the deacon does.

240. While the *Agnus Dei* is sung or said, the deacons or some of the concelebrants may help the principal celebrant break the hosts for Communion, both of the concelebrants and of the people.

241. After the commingling, the principal celebrant alone, with hands joined, privately says the prayer *Domine Iesu Christe, Fili Dei vivi* (*Lord Jesus Christ, Son of the living God*) or *Perceptio Corporis et Sanguinis* (*Lord Jesus Christ, with faith in your love and mercy*).

242. When this prayer before Communion is finished, the principal celebrant genuflects and steps back a little. Then one after another the concelebrants come to the middle of the altar, genuflect, and reverently take

the Body of Christ from the altar. Then holding it in their right hand, with the left hand placed below, they return to their places. The concelebrants may, however, remain in their places and take the Body of Christ from the paten presented to them by the principal celebrant or by one or more of the concelebrants, or by passing the paten one to another.

243. Then the principal celebrant takes a host consecrated in the same Mass, holds it slightly raised above the paten or the chalice, and, facing the people, says the *Ecce Agnus Dei* (*This is the Lamb of God*). With the concelebrants and the people he continues, saying the *Domine, non sum dignus* (*Lord, I am not worthy*).

244. Then the principal celebrant, facing the altar, says quietly, *Corpus Christi custodiat me ad vitam aeternam* (*May the body of Christ bring me to everlasting life*), and reverently receives the Body of Christ. The concelebrants do likewise, communicating themselves. After them the deacon receives the Body and Blood of the Lord from the principal celebrant.

245. The Blood of the Lord may be received either by drinking from the chalice directly, or by intinction, or by means of a tube or a spoon.

246. If Communion is received by drinking directly from the chalice, one or other of two procedures may be followed:

    a.   The principal celebrant, standing at the middle of the altar, takes the chalice and says quietly, *Sanguis Christi custodiat me in vitam aeternam* (*May the Blood of Christ bring me to everlasting life*). He consumes a little of the Blood of Christ and hands the chalice to the deacon or a concelebrant. He then distributes Communion to the faithful (cf. nos. 160-162).

        The concelebrants approach the altar one after another or, if two chalices are used, two by two. They genuflect, partake of the Blood of Christ, wipe the rim of the chalice, and return to their seats.

b. The principal celebrant normally consumes the Blood of the Lord standing at the middle of the altar.

The concelebrants may, however, partake of the Blood of the Lord while remaining in their places and drinking from the chalice presented to them by the deacon or by one of the concelebrants, or else passed from one to the other. The chalice is always wiped either by the one who drinks from it or by the one who presents it. After communicating, each returns to his seat.

247. The deacon reverently drinks at the altar all of the Blood of Christ that remains, assisted, if necessary, by some of the concelebrants. He then carries the chalice over to the credence table and there he or a duly instituted acolyte purifies, wipes, and arranges it in the usual way (cf. no. 183).

248. The Communion of the concelebrants may also be arranged so that each concelebrant communicates the Body of the Lord at the altar and, immediately afterwards, the Blood of the Lord.

In this case the principal celebrant receives Communion under both kinds in the usual way (cf. no. 158), observing, however, the rite chosen in each particular instance for Communion from the chalice; and the other concelebrants should follow suit.

After the principal celebrant's Communion, the chalice is placed on another corporal at the side of the altar. The concelebrants approach the middle of the altar one after another, genuflect, and receive the Body of the Lord; then they go to the side of the altar and consume the Blood of the Lord, following the rite chosen for Communion from the chalice, as has just been said.

The Communion of the deacon and the purification of the chalice take place as already described.

249. If the concelebrants' Communion is by intinction, the principal celebrant receives the Body and Blood of the Lord in the usual way, but making sure that enough of the precious Blood remains in the chalice for the Communion of the concelebrants. Then the deacon, or one of the concelebrants, arranges the chalice as appropriate in the center of the altar or at the side on another corporal together with the paten containing particles of the host.

The concelebrants approach the altar one after another, genuflect, and take a particle, dip it partly into the chalice, and, holding a purificator under their chin, consume the intincted particle. They then return to their places as at the beginning of Mass.

The deacon also receives Communion by intinction and to the concelebrant's words, *Corpus et Sanguis Christi* (*The Body and Blood of Christ*) makes the response, *Amen*. The deacon, however, consumes at the altar all that remains of the Precious Blood, assisted, if necessary, by some of the concelebrants. He carries the chalice to the credence table and there he or a duly instituted acolyte purifies, wipes and arranges it in the usual way.

The Concluding Rites
250. Everything else is done by the principal celebrant in the usual way until the end of Mass (cf. nos. 166-168), while the other concelebrants remain at their seats.

251. Before leaving the altar, the concelebrants make a profound bow to the altar. For his part the principal celebrant, along with the deacon, venerates the altar with a kiss in the usual way.

III. MASS AT WHICH ONLY ONE MINISTER PARTICIPATES

252. At a Mass celebrated by a priest with only one minister to assist him and to make the responses, the rite of Mass with a congregation is followed (cf. nos. 120-169) the minister saying the people's parts as appropriate.

253. If, however, the minister is a deacon, he performs his proper duties (cf. nos. 171-186) and likewise carries out the other parts, that is, those of the people.

254. Mass should not be celebrated without a minister or at least one of the faithful, except for a just and reasonable cause. In this case, the greetings, the introductory or explanatory remarks, and the blessing at the end of Mass are omitted.

255. Before Mass, the necessary vessels are prepared either at the credence table or on the righthand side of the altar.

The Introductory Rites

256. The priest approaches the altar and, after making a profound bow along with the minister, venerates the altar with a kiss and goes to the chair. If he wishes, the priest may remain at the altar; in this case, the Missal is likewise prepared there. Then the minister or the priest says the Entrance Antiphon.

257. Then the priest, standing, makes with the minister the sign of the Cross as the priest says, *In nomine Patris* (*In the name of the Father*). Facing the minister, he greets the minister choosing one of the formulas of greeting.

258. Then the Act of Penitence takes place, and, if required by the rubrics, the *Kyrie* and *Gloria* are said.

259. Then, with hands joined, the priest says, *Oremus* (*Let us pray*). After a suitable pause, with hands extended he says the collect. At the end the minister makes the acclamation, *Amen*.

The Liturgy of the Word
260. The readings should whenever possible be proclaimed from the ambo or a lectern.

261. After the collect, the minister reads the first reading and Psalm, the second reading, when it is to be said, and the verse for the *Alleluia* or other chant.

262. Then the priest bows profoundly and says the *Munda cor meum* (*Almighty God, cleanse my heart*) and, afterwards, reads the Gospel. At the conclusion he says, *Verbum Domini* (*The Gospel of the Lord*), to which the minister responds, *Laus tibi, Christe* (*Praise to you, Lord Jesus Christ*). The priest then venerates the book with a kiss, saying quietly the *Per evangelica dicta* (*May the words of the Gospel*).

263. Afterwards, if required by the rubrics, the priest says the Creed together with the minister.

264. The Prayer of the Faithful follows, which may be said even in this form of Mass. The priest introduces and concludes it, with the minister announcing the intentions.

The Liturgy of the Eucharist
265. In the Liturgy of the Eucharist, everything is done as in a Mass with a congregation, with the following exceptions.

266. After the acclamation at the end of the embolism that follows the Lord's Prayer, the priest says the prayer *Domine Iesu Christe, qui dixisti* (*Lord Jesus Christ, you said*). He then adds, *Pax Domini sit semper vobiscum* (*The peace of the Lord be with you always*), and the minister

answers, *Et cum spiritu tuo* (*And also with you*). The priest gives the sign of peace to the minister, if appropriate.

267. Then, while he says the *Agnus Dei* (*Lamb of God*) with the minister, the priest breaks the host over the paten. After the *Agnus Dei*, he performs the commingling, saying quietly the *Haec commixtio* (*May this mingling*).

268. After the commingling, the priest quietly says the prayer *Domine Iesu Christe, Fili Dei vivi* (*Lord Jesus Christ, Son of the living God*) or *Perceptio* (*Lord Jesus Christ, with faith in your love and mercy*). Then he genuflects, takes the host, and, if the minister is to receive Communion, turns to the minister and, holding the host a little above the paten or the chalice, says the *Ecce Agnus Dei* (*This is the Lamb of God*), adding with the minister the *Domine, non sum dignus* (*Lord, I am not worthy*). Facing the altar, the priest then partakes of the Body of Christ. If, however, the minister does not receive Communion, the priest, after genuflecting, takes the host and, facing the altar, says quietly the *Domine, non sum dignus* (*Lord, I am not worthy*) and the *Corpus Christi custodiat* (*May the Body of Christ bring*) and then receives the Body of Christ. Then he takes the chalice and says quietly, *Sanguis Christi custodiat* (*May the Blood of Christ bring*), and then consumes the Blood of Christ.

269. Before Communion is given to the minister, the Communion Antiphon is said by the minister or by the priest himself.

270. The priest purifies the chalice at the credence table or at the altar. If the chalice is purified at the altar, it may be carried to the credence table by the minister or may again be placed on the altar at the side.

271. After the purification of the chalice, the priest should observe some moments of silence, after which he says the prayer after Communion.

The Concluding Rites

272. The concluding rites are carried out as at a Mass with a congregation, but the dismissal formula is omitted. The priest venerates the altar in the usual way with a kiss and, after making a profound bow with the minister, departs.

IV. SOME GENERAL NORMS FOR ALL FORMS OF MASS

Veneration of the Altar and the Book of the Gospels

273. According to traditional practice, the altar and the *Book of the Gospels* are venerated by means of a kiss. Where, however, a sign of this kind is not in harmony with the traditions or the culture of some region, it is for the Conference of Bishops to establish some other sign in its place, with the consent of the Apostolic See.

Genuflections and Bows

274. A genuflection, made by bending the right knee to the ground, signifies adoration, and therefore it is reserved for the Most Blessed Sacrament, as well as for the Holy Cross from the solemn adoration during the liturgical celebration on Good Friday until the beginning of the Easter Vigil.

During Mass, three genuflections are made by the priest celebrant: namely, after the showing of the host, after the showing of the chalice, and before Communion. Certain specific features to be observed in a concelebrated Mass are noted in their proper place (cf. nos. 210-251).

If, however, the tabernacle with the Most Blessed Sacrament is present in the sanctuary, the priest, the deacon, and the other ministers genuflect when they approach the altar and when they depart from it, but not during the celebration of Mass itself.

Otherwise all who pass before the Most Blessed Sacrament genuflect, unless they are moving in procession.

Ministers carrying the processional cross or candles bow their heads instead of genuflecting.

275. A bow signifies reverence and honor shown to the persons themselves or to the signs that represent them. There are two kinds of bows: a bow of the head and a bow of the body.

    a.   A bow of the head is made when the three Divine Persons are named together and at the names of Jesus, of the Blessed Virgin Mary, and of the Saint in whose honor Mass is being celebrated.

    b.   A bow of the body, that is to say a profound bow, is made to the altar; during the prayers *Munda cor meum* (*Almighty God, cleanse my heart*) and *In spiritu humilitatis* (*Lord God, we ask you to receive*); in the Creed at the words *Et incarnatus est* (*by the power of the Holy Spirit . . . and became man*); in the Roman Canon at the words *Supplices te rogamus* (*Almighty God, we pray that your angel*). The same kind of bow is made by the deacon when he asks for a blessing before the proclamation of the Gospel. In addition, the priest bows slightly as he speaks the words of the Lord at the consecration.

Incensation

276. Thurification or incensation is an expression of reverence and of prayer, as is signified in Sacred Scripture (cf. Ps 141 [140]:2, Rev 8:3).

Incense may be used if desired in any form of Mass:

    a.   During the Entrance procession;
    b.   At the beginning of Mass, to incense the cross and the altar;
    c.   At the Gospel procession and the proclamation of the Gospel itself;
    d.   After the bread and the chalice have been placed upon the altar, to incense the offerings, the cross, and the altar, as well as the priest and the people;
    e.   At the showing of the host and the chalice after the consecration.

277. The priest, having put incense into the thurible, blesses it with the sign of the Cross, without saying anything.

Before and after an incensation, a profound bow is made to the person or object that is incensed, except for the incensation of the altar and the offerings for the Sacrifice of the Mass.

The following are incensed with three swings of the thurible: the Most Blessed Sacrament, a relic of the Holy Cross and images of the Lord exposed for public veneration, the offerings for the sacrifice of the Mass, the altar cross, the *Book of the Gospels*, the Paschal Candle, the priest, and the people.

The following are incensed with two swings of the thurible: relics and images of the Saints exposed for public veneration, which should be done, however, only at the beginning of the celebration, after the incensation of the altar.

The altar is incensed with single swings of the thurible in this way:

    a. If the altar is freestanding with respect to the wall, the priest incenses walking around it;

    b. If the altar is not freestanding, the priest incenses it while walking first to the righthand side, then to the left.

The cross, if situated on or near the altar, is incensed by the priest before he incenses the altar; otherwise, he incenses it when he passes in front of it.

The priest incenses the offerings with three swings of the thurible or by making the sign of the cross over the offerings with the thurible before going on to incense the cross and the altar.

The Purification
278. Whenever a fragment of the host adheres to his fingers, especially after the fraction or the Communion of the faithful, the priest is to wipe his fingers over the paten or, if necessary, wash them. Likewise, he should also gather any fragments that may have fallen outside the paten.

279. The sacred vessels are purified by the priest, the deacon, or an instituted acolyte after Communion or after Mass, insofar as possible at the credence table. The purification of the chalice is done with water alone or with wine and water, which is then drunk by whoever does the purification. The paten is usually wiped clean with the purificator.

Care must be taken that whatever may remain of the Blood of Christ after the distribution of Communion is consumed immediately and completely at the altar.

280. If a host or any particle should fall, it is to be picked up reverently. If any of the Precious Blood is spilled, the area where the spill occurred should be washed with water, and this water should then be poured into the sacrarium in the sacristy.

Communion under Both Kinds
281. Holy Communion has a fuller form as a sign when it is distributed under both kinds. For in this form the sign of the Eucharistic banquet is more clearly evident and clear expression is given to the divine will by which the new and eternal Covenant is ratified in the Blood of the Lord, as also the relationship between the Eucharistic banquet and the eschatological banquet in the Father's Kingdom.[105]

282. Sacred pastors should take care to ensure that the faithful who participate in the rite or are present at it are as fully aware as possible of the

---

105   Cf. Sacred Congregation of Rites, Instruction *Eucharisticum mysterium*, On the worship of the Eucharist, 25 May 1967, no. 32: AAS 59 (1967), p. 558.

Catholic teaching on the form of Holy Communion as set forth by the Ecumenical Council of Trent. Above all, they should instruct the Christian faithful that the Catholic faith teaches that Christ, whole and entire, and the true Sacrament, is received even under only one species, and consequently that as far as the effects are concerned, those who receive under only one species are not deprived of any of the grace that is necessary for salvation.[106]

They are to teach, furthermore, that the Church, in her stewardship of the Sacraments, has the power to set forth or alter whatever provisions, apart from the substance of the Sacraments, that she judges to be most conducive to the veneration of the Sacraments and the well-being of the recipients, in view of changing conditions, times, and places.[107] At the same time, the faithful should be encouraged to seek to participate more eagerly in this sacred rite, by which the sign of the Eucharistic banquet is made more fully evident.

283. In addition to those cases given in the ritual books, Communion under both kinds is permitted for

    a.   Priests who are not able to celebrate or concelebrate Mass;
    b.   The deacon and others who perform some duty at the Mass;
    c.   Members of communities at the conventual Mass or "community" Mass, along with seminarians, and all who are engaged in a retreat or are taking part in a spiritual or pastoral gathering.

The diocesan Bishop may establish norms for Communion under both kinds for his own diocese, which are also to be observed in churches of religious and at celebrations with small groups. The diocesan Bishop is

---

106   Cf. Council of Trent, session 21, *Doctrina de communione sub utraque specie et parvulorum*, 16 July 1562, chapters 1-3: Denz-Schön, 1725-1729.

107   Cf. Council of Trent, session 21, *Doctrina de communione sub utraque specie et parvulorum*, chapter 2: Denz-Schön, 1728.

also given the faculty to permit Communion under both kinds whenever it may seem appropriate to the priest to whom, as its own shepherd, a community has been entrusted, provided that the faithful have been well instructed and there is no danger of profanation of the Sacrament or of the rite's becoming difficult because of the large number of participants or some other reason.

In all that pertains to Communion under both kinds, the *Norms for the Distribution and Reception of Holy Communion under Both Kinds in the Dioceses of the United States of America* are to be followed (see nos. 27-54).

284. When Communion is distributed under both kinds,

  a. The chalice is usually administered by a deacon or, when no deacon is present, by a priest, or even by a duly instituted acolyte or another extraordinary minister of Holy Communion, or by a member of the faithful who, in case of necessity, has been entrusted with this duty for a single occasion;
  b. Whatever may remain of the Blood of Christ is consumed at the altar by the priest or the deacon or the duly instituted acolyte who ministered the chalice. The same then purifies, wipes, and arranges the sacred vessels in the usual way.

Any of the faithful who wish to receive Holy Communion under the species of bread alone should be granted their wish.

285. For Communion under both kinds the following should be prepared:

  a. If Communion from the chalice is carried out by communicants' drinking directly from the chalice, a chalice of a sufficiently large size or several chalices are prepared. Care should, however, be taken in planning lest beyond what is needed of the Blood of Christ remains to be consumed at the end of the celebration.

  b. If Communion is carried out by intinction, the hosts should be neither too thin nor too small, but rather a little thicker than usual, so that after being dipped partly into the Blood of Christ they can still easily be distributed to each communicant.

286. If Communion of the Blood of Christ is carried out by communicants' drinking from the chalice, each communicant, after receiving the Body of Christ, moves and stands facing the minister of the chalice. The minister says, *Sanguis Christi* (*The Blood of Christ*), the communicant responds, *Amen,* and the minister hands over the chalice, which the communicant raises to his or her mouth. Each communicant drinks a little from the chalice, hands it back to the minister, and then withdraws; the minister wipes the rim of the chalice with the purificator.

287. If Communion from the chalice is carried out by intinction, each communicant, holding a communion-plate under the chin, approaches the priest who holds a vessel with the sacred particles, a minister standing at his side and holding the chalice. The priest takes a host, dips it partly into the chalice and, showing it, says, *Corpus et Sanguis Christi* (*The Body and Blood of Christ*). The communicant responds, *Amen,* receives the Sacrament in the mouth from the priest, and then withdraws.

CHAPTER V
The Arrangement and Furnishing of Churches for the Celebration of the Eucharist

I. GENERAL PRINCIPLES

288. For the celebration of the Eucharist, the people of God normally are gathered together in a church or, if there is no church or if it is too small, then in another respectable place that is nonetheless worthy of so great a mystery. Churches, therefore, and other places should be suitable for carrying out the sacred action and for ensuring the active participation of the faithful. Sacred buildings and requisites for divine worship should, moreover, be truly worthy and beautiful and be signs and symbols of heavenly realities.[108]

289. Consequently, the Church constantly seeks the noble assistance of the arts and admits the artistic expressions of all peoples and regions.[109] In fact, just as she is intent on preserving the works of art and the artistic treasures handed down from past centuries[110] and, insofar as necessary, on

---

108 Cf. Second Vatican Ecumenical Council, Constitution on the Sacred Liturgy, *Sacrosanctum Concilium*, nos. 122-124; Decree on the Ministry and Life of Priests, *Presbyterorum ordinis*, no. 5; Sacred Congregation of Rites, Instruction *Inter Oecumenici*, On the orderly carrying out of the Constitution on the Sacred Liturgy, 26 September 1964, no. 90: AAS 56 (1964), p. 897; Sacred Congregation of Rites, Instruction *Eucharisticum mysterium*, On the worship of the Eucharist, 25 May 1967, no. 24: AAS 59 (1967), p. 554; *Codex Iuris Canonici*, can. 932 § 1.

109 Cf. Second Vatican Ecumenical Council, Constitution on the Sacred Liturgy, *Sacrosanctum Concilium*, no. 123.

110 Cf. Sacred Congregation of Rites, Instruction *Eucharisticum mysterium*, On the worship of the Eucharist, 25 May 1967, no. 24: AAS 59 (1967), p. 554.

adapting them to new needs, so also she strives to promote new works of art that are in harmony with the character of each successive age.[111]

On account of this, in commissioning artists and choosing works of art to be admitted into a church, what should be required is that true excellence in art which nourishes faith and devotion and accords authentically with both the meaning and the purpose for which it is intended.[112]

290. All churches should be dedicated or, at least, blessed. Cathedrals and parish churches, however, are to be dedicated with a solemn rite.

291. For the proper construction, restoration, and remodeling of sacred buildings, all who are involved in the work are to consult the diocesan commission on the sacred Liturgy and sacred Art. The diocesan Bishop, moreover, should use the counsel and help of this commission whenever it comes to laying down norms on this matter, approving plans for new buildings, and making decisions on the more important issues.[113]

292. Church decor should contribute toward the church's noble simplicity rather than ostentation. In the choice of materials for church appointments there should be a concern for genuineness of materials and an intent to foster the instruction of the faithful and the dignity of the entire sacred place.

---

111   Cf. Second Vatican Ecumenical Council, Constitution on the Sacred Liturgy, *Sacrosanctum Concilium*, nos. 123, 129; Sacred Congregation of Rites, Instruction *Inter Oecumenici*, On the orderly carrying out of the Constitution on the Sacred Liturgy, 26 September 1964, no. 13c: AAS 56 (1964), p. 880.

112   Cf. Second Vatican Ecumenical Council, Constitution on the Sacred Liturgy, *Sacrosanctum Concilium*, no. 123.

113   Cf. Second Vatican Ecumenical Council, Constitution on the Sacred Liturgy, *Sacrosanctum Concilium*, no. 126; Sacred Congregation of Rites, Instruction *Inter Oecumenici*, On the orderly carrying out of the Constitution on the Sacred Liturgy, 26 September 1964, no. 91: AAS 56 (1964), p. 898.

293. A proper arrangement of a church and its surroundings that appropriately meets contemporary needs requires attention not only to the elements related more directly to the celebration of the sacred actions but also to those things conducive to the appropriate comfort of the faithful that are normally forthcoming in places where people regularly gather.

294. The People of God, gathered for Mass, has a coherent and hierarchical structure, which finds its expression in the variety of ministries and the variety of actions according to the different parts of the celebration. The general ordering of the sacred building must be such that in some way it conveys the image of the gathered assembly and allows the appropriate ordering of all the participants, as well as facilitating each in the proper carrying out of his function.

The faithful and the choir should have a place that facilitates their active participation.[114]

The priest celebrant, the deacon, and the other ministers have places in the sanctuary. Seats for concelebrants should also be prepared there. If, however, their number is great, seats should be arranged in another part of the church, but near the altar.

All these elements, even though they must express the hierarchical structure and the diversity of ministries, should nevertheless bring about a close and coherent unity that is clearly expressive of the unity of the entire holy people. Indeed, the character and beauty of the place and all its furnishings should foster devotion and show forth the holiness of the mysteries celebrated there.

---

114   Cf. Sacred Congregation of Rites, Instruction *Inter Oecumenici*, On the orderly carrying out of the Constitution on the Sacred Liturgy, 26 September 1964, nos. 97-98: AAS 56 (1964), p. 899.

II. ARRANGEMENT OF THE SANCTUARY FOR THE SACRED SYNAXIS (EUCHARISTIC ASSEMBLY)

295. The sanctuary is the place where the altar stands, where the word of God is proclaimed, and where the priest, the deacon, and the other ministers exercise their offices. It should suitably be marked off from the body of the church either by its being somewhat elevated or by a particular structure and ornamentation. It should, however, be large enough to allow the Eucharist to be celebrated properly and easily seen.[115]

The Altar and Its Appointments

296. The altar on which the Sacrifice of the Cross is made present under sacramental signs is also the table of the Lord to which the People of God is called together to participate in the Mass, as well as the center of the thanksgiving that is accomplished through the Eucharist.

297. The celebration of the Eucharist in a sacred place is to be carried out on an altar; but outside a sacred place, it may be carried out on a suitable table, always with the use of a cloth, a corporal, a cross, and candles.

298. It is appropriate to have a fixed altar in every church, since it more clearly and permanently signifies Christ Jesus, the living stone (1 Pt 2:4; cf. Eph 2:20). In other places set aside for sacred celebrations, the altar may be movable.

An altar is called "fixed" if it is attached to the floor so as not to be removeable; otherwise it is called "moveable."

299. The altar should be built apart from the wall, in such a way that it is possible to walk around it easily and that Mass can be celebrated at it facing the people, which is desirable wherever possible. The altar should, moreover, be so placed as to be truly the center toward which

---

115   Cf. Sacred Congregation of Rites, Instruction *Inter Oecumenici*, On the orderly carrying out of the Constitution on the Sacred Liturgy, 26 September 1964, no. 91: AAS 56 (1964), p. 898.

the attention of the whole congregation of the faithful naturally turns.[116] The altar is usually fixed and is dedicated.

300. An altar whether fixed or movable is dedicated according to the rite prescribed in the Roman Pontifical; but it is permissible for a movable altar simply to be blessed.

301. In keeping with the Church's traditional practice and the altar's symbolism, the table of a fixed altar is to be of stone and indeed of natural stone. In the dioceses of the United States of America, however, wood which is worthy, solid, and well-crafted may be used, provided that the altar is structurally immobile. The supports or base for upholding the table, however, may be made of any sort of material, provided it is worthy and solid.

A movable altar may be constructed of any noble and solid materials suited to liturgical use, according to the traditions and usages of the different regions.

302. The practice of placing relics of Saints, even those not Martyrs, under the altar to be dedicated is fittingly retained. Care should be taken, however, to ensure the authenticity of such relics.

303. In building new churches, it is preferable to erect a single altar which in the gathering of the faithful will signify the one Christ and the one Eucharist of the Church.

In already existing churches, however, when the old altar is positioned so that it makes the people's participation difficult but cannot be moved without damage to its artistic value, another fixed altar, of artistic merit and duly dedicated, should be erected and sacred rites celebrated on it

116   Cf. Sacred Congregation of Rites, Instruction *Inter Oecumenici*, On the orderly carrying out of the Constitution on the Sacred Liturgy, 26 September 1964, no. 91: AAS 56 (1964), p. 898.

alone. In order not to distract the attention of the faithful from the new altar, the old altar should not be decorated in any special way.

304. Out of reverence for the celebration of the memorial of the Lord and for the banquet in which the Body and Blood of the Lord are offered on an altar where this memorial is celebrated, there should be at least one white cloth, its shape, size, and decoration in keeping with the altar's design. When, in the dioceses of the United States of America, other cloths are used in addition to the altar cloth, then those cloths may be of other colors possessing Christian honorific or festive significance according to longstanding local usage, provided that the uppermost cloth covering the *mensa* (i.e., the altar cloth itself) is always white in color.

305. Moderation should be observed in the decoration of the altar.

During Advent the floral decoration of the altar should be marked by a moderation suited to the character of this season, without expressing prematurely the full joy of the Nativity of the Lord. During Lent it is forbidden for the altar to be decorated with flowers. *Laetare* Sunday (Fourth Sunday of Lent), solemnities, and feasts are exceptions.

Floral decorations should always be done with moderation and placed around the altar rather than on its *mensa*.

306. Only what is required for the celebration of the Mass may be placed on the *mensa* of the altar: namely, from the beginning of the celebration until the proclamation of the Gospel, the *Book of the Gospels*; then from the Presentation of the Gifts until the purification of the vessels, the chalice with the paten, a ciborium, if necessary, and, finally, the corporal, the purificator, the pall, and the Missal.

In addition, microphones that may be needed to amplify the priest's voice should be arranged discreetly.

307. The candles, which are required at every liturgical service out of reverence and on account of the festiveness of the celebration (cf. no. 117), are to be appropriately placed either on or around the altar in a way suited to the design of the altar and the sanctuary so that the whole may be well balanced and not interfere with the faithful's clear view of what takes place at the altar or what is placed on it.

308. There is also to be a cross, with the figure of Christ crucified upon it, either on the altar or near it, where it is clearly visible to the assembled congregation. It is appropriate that such a cross, which calls to mind for the faithful the saving Passion of the Lord, remain near the altar even outside of liturgical celebrations.

The Ambo
309. The dignity of the word of God requires that the church have a place that is suitable for the proclamation of the word and toward which the attention of the whole congregation of the faithful naturally turns during the Liturgy of the Word.[117]

It is appropriate that this place be ordinarily a stationary ambo and not simply a movable lectern. The ambo must be located in keeping with the design of each church in such a way that the ordained ministers and lectors may be clearly seen and heard by the faithful.

From the ambo only the readings, the responsorial Psalm, and the Easter Proclamation (*Exsultet*) are to be proclaimed; it may be used also for giving the homily and for announcing the intentions of the Prayer of the Faithful. The dignity of the ambo requires that only a minister of the word should go up to it.

---

117   Cf. Sacred Congregation of Rites, Instruction *Inter Oecumenici*, On the orderly carrying out of the Constitution on the Sacred Liturgy, 26 September 1964, no. 92: AAS 56 (1964), p. 899.

It is appropriate that a new ambo be blessed according to the rite described in the Roman Ritual[118] before it is put into liturgical use.

The Chair for the Priest Celebrant and Other Seats

310. The chair of the priest celebrant must signify his office of presiding over the gathering and of directing the prayer. Thus the best place for the chair is in a position facing the people at the head of the sanctuary, unless the design of the building or other circumstances impede this: for example, if the great distance would interfere with communication between the priest and the gathered assembly, or if the tabernacle is in the center behind the altar. Any appearance of a throne, however, is to be avoided.[119] It is appropriate that, before being put into liturgical use, the chair be blessed according to the rite described in the Roman Ritual.[120]

Likewise, seats should be arranged in the sanctuary for concelebrating priests as well as for priests who are present for the celebration in choir dress but who are not concelebrating.

The seat for the deacon should be placed near that of the celebrant. Seats for the other ministers are to be arranged so that they are clearly distinguishable from those for the clergy and so that the ministers are easily able to fulfill the function entrusted to them.[121]

---

118   Cf. The Roman Ritual, *Book of Blessings, editio typica*, 1984, Order for a Blessing on the Occasion of the Installation of a New Ambo, nos. 900-918.

119   Cf. Sacred Congregation of Rites, Instruction *Inter Oecumenici*, On the orderly carrying out of the Constitution on the Sacred Liturgy, 26 September 1964, no 92: AAS 56 (1964), p. 898.

120   Cf. The Roman Ritual, *Book of Blessings, editio typica*, 1984, Order for a Blessing on the Occasion of the Installation of a New Cathedra or Presidential Chair, nos. 880-899.

121   Cf. Sacred Congregation of Rites, Instruction *Inter Oecumenici*, On the orderly carrying out of the Constitution on the Sacred Liturgy, 26 September 1964, no. 92: AAS 56 (1964), p. 898.

III. THE ARRANGEMENT OF THE CHURCH

The Places for the Faithful

311. Places should be arranged with appropriate care for the faithful so that they are able to participate in the sacred celebrations visually and spiritually, in the proper manner. It is expedient for benches or seats usually to be provided for their use. The custom of reserving seats for private persons, however, is reprehensible.[122] Moreover, benches or chairs should be arranged, especially in newly built churches, in such a way that the people can easily take up the postures required for the different parts of the celebration and can easily come forward to receive Holy Communion.

Care should be taken that the faithful be able not only to see the priest, the deacon, and the lectors but also, with the aid of modern technical means, to hear them without difficulty.

The Place for the Choir and the Musical Instruments

312. The choir should be positioned with respect to the design of each church so as to make clearly evident its character as a part of the gathered community of the faithful fulfilling a specific function. The location should also assist the choir to exercise its function more easily and conveniently allow each choir member full, sacramental participation in the Mass.[123]

313. The organ and other lawfully approved musical instruments are to be placed in an appropriate place so that they can sustain the singing of both the choir and the congregation and be heard with ease by all if they are played alone. It is appropriate that, before being put into liturgical use, the organ be blessed according to the rite described in the Roman Ritual.[124]

---

122 Cf. Second Vatican Ecumenical Council, Constitution on the Sacred Liturgy, *Sacrosanctum Concilium*, no. 32.

123 Cf. Sacred Congregation of Rites, Instruction *Musicam sacram*, On music in the Liturgy, 5 March 1967, no. 23: AAS 59 (1967), p. 307.

124 Cf. The Roman Ritual, *Book of Blessings, editio typica*, 1984, Order for the Blessing of an Organ, nos. 1052-1067.

In Advent the organ and other musical instruments should be used with a moderation that is consistent with the season's character and does not anticipate the full joy of the Nativity of the Lord.

In Lent the playing of the organ and musical instruments is allowed only to support the singing. Exceptions are *Laetare* Sunday (Fourth Sunday of Lent), solemnities, and feasts.

The Place for the Reservation of the Most Holy Eucharist
314. In accordance with the structure of each church and legitimate local customs, the Most Blessed Sacrament should be reserved in a tabernacle in a part of the church that is truly noble, prominent, readily visible, beautifully decorated, and suitable for prayer.[125]

The one tabernacle should be immovable, be made of solid and inviolable material that is not transparent, and be locked in such a way that the danger of profanation is prevented to the greatest extent possible.[126] Moreover, it is appropriate that, before it is put into liturgical use, it be blessed according to the rite described in the Roman Ritual.[127]

---

125   Cf. Sacred Congregation of Rites, Instruction *Eucharisticum mysterium*, On the worship of the Eucharist, 25 May 1967, no. 54: AAS 59 (1967), p. 568; cf. also Sacred Congregation of Rites, Instruction *Inter Oecumenici*, On the orderly carrying out of the Constitution on the Sacred Liturgy, 26 September 1964, no. 95: AAS 56 (1964), p. 898.

126   Cf. Sacred Congregation of Rites, Instruction *Eucharisticum mysterium*, On the worship of the Eucharist, 25 May 1967. no. 52: AAS 59 (1967), p. 568; Sacred Congregation of Rites, Instruction *Inter Oecumenici*, On the orderly carrying out of the Constitution on the Sacred Liturgy, 26 September 1964, no. 95: AAS 56 (1964), p. 898; Sacred Congregation for the Sacraments, Instruction *Nullo umquam tempore*, 28 May 1938, no. 4: AAS 30 (1938), pp. 199-200; The Roman Ritual, *Holy Communion and Worship of the Eucharist outside Mass, editio typica*, 1973, nos. 10-11; *Codex Iuris Canonici*, can. 938 § 3.

127   Cf. The Roman Ritual, *Book of Blessings, editio typica*, 1984, Order for a Blessing on the Occasion of the Installation of a New Tabernacle, nos. 919-929.

315. It is more in keeping with the meaning of the sign that the tabernacle in which the Most Holy Eucharist is reserved not be on an altar on which Mass is celebrated.[128]

Consequently, it is preferable that the tabernacle be located, according to the judgment of the diocesan Bishop,

    a.   Either in the sanctuary, apart from the altar of celebration, in a form and place more appropriate, not excluding on an old altar no longer used for celebration (cf. no. 303);

    b.   Or even in some chapel suitable for the faithful's private adoration and prayer[129] and organically connected to the church and readily visible to the Christian faithful.

316. In accordance with traditional custom, near the tabernacle a special lamp, fueled by oil or wax, should be kept alight to indicate and honor the presence of Christ.[130]

---

128   Cf. Sacred Congregation of Rites, Instruction *Eucharisticum mysterium*, On the worship of the Eucharist, 25 May 1967. no. 55: AAS 59 (1967), p. 569.

129   Cf. Sacred Congregation of Rites, Instruction *Eucharisticum mysterium*, On the worship of the Eucharist, 25 May 1967, no. 53: AAS 59 (1967), p. 568; The Roman Ritual, *Holy Communion and Worship of the Eucharist outside Mass, editio typica*, 1973, no. 9; *Codex Iuris Canonici*, can. 938 § 2; John Paul II, Apostolic Letter *Dominicae Cenae*, 24 February 1980, no. 3: AAS 72 (1980), pp. 117-119.

130   Cf. *Codex Iuris Canonici*, can. 940; Sacred Congregation of Rites, Instruction *Eucharisticum mysterium*, On the worship of the Eucharist, 25 May 1967, no. 57: AAS 59 (1967), p. 569; The Roman Ritual, *Holy Communion and Worship of the Eucharist outside Mass, editio typica*, 1973, no. 11.

317. In no way should all the other things prescribed by law concerning the reservation of the Most Holy Eucharist be forgotten.[131]

Sacred Images

318. In the earthly Liturgy, the Church participates, by a foretaste, in that heavenly Liturgy which is celebrated in the holy city of Jerusalem toward which she journeys as a pilgrim, and where Christ is sitting at the right hand of God; and by venerating the memory of the Saints, she hopes one day to have some part and fellowship with them.[132]

Thus, images of the Lord, the Blessed Virgin Mary, and the Saints, in accordance with the Church's most ancient tradition, should be displayed for veneration by the faithful in sacred buildings[133] and should be arranged so as to usher the faithful toward the mysteries of faith celebrated there. For this reason, care should be taken that their number not be increased indiscriminately, and that they be arranged in proper order so as not to distract the faithful's attention from the celebration itself.[134] There should usually be only one image of any given Saint. Generally speaking, in the ornamentation and arrangement of a church as far as images are concerned, provision should be made for the devotion of the entire community as well as for the beauty and dignity of the images.

---

131   Cf. particularly in Sacred Congregation for the Sacraments, Instruction *Nullo umquam tempore*, 28 May 1938: AAS 30 (1938), pp. 198-207; *Codex Iuris Canonici*, cann. 934-944.

132   Cf. Second Vatican Ecumenical Council, Constitution on the Sacred Liturgy, *Sacrosanctum Concilium*, no. 8.

133   Cf. The Roman Pontifical: *Order of the Dedication of a Church and an Altar, editio typica*, 1984, Chapter 4, no. 10; The Roman Ritual, *Book of Blessings, editio typica*, 1984, Order for the Blessing of Images for Public Veneration by the Faithful, nos. 984-1031.

134   Cf. Second Vatican Ecumenical Council, Constitution on the Sacred Liturgy, *Sacrosanctum Concilium*, no. 125.

CHAPTER VI
The Requisites for the Celebration of Mass

I. THE BREAD AND WINE FOR
CELEBRATING THE EUCHARIST

319. Following the example of Christ, the Church has always used bread and wine with water to celebrate the Lord's Supper.

320. The bread for celebrating the Eucharist must be made only from wheat, must be recently baked, and, according to the ancient tradition of the Latin Church, must be unleavened.

321. The meaning of the sign demands that the material for the Eucharistic celebration truly have the appearance of food. It is therefore expedient that the Eucharistic bread, even though unleavened and baked in the traditional shape, be made in such a way that the priest at Mass with a congregation is able in practice to break it into parts for distribution to at least some of the faithful. Small hosts are, however, in no way ruled out when the number of those receiving Holy Communion or other pastoral needs require it. The action of the fraction or breaking of bread, which gave its name to the Eucharist in apostolic times, will bring out more clearly the force and importance of the sign of unity of all in the one bread, and of the sign of charity by the fact that the one bread is distributed among the brothers and sisters.

322. The wine for the Eucharistic celebration must be from the fruit of the grapevine (cf. Lk 22:18), natural, and unadulterated, that is, without admixture of extraneous substances.

323. Diligent care should be taken to ensure that the bread and wine intended for the Eucharist are kept in a perfect state of conservation: that is, that the wine does not turn to vinegar nor the bread spoil or become too hard to be broken easily.

324. If the priest notices after the consecration or as he receives Communion that not wine but only water was poured into the chalice, he pours the water into some container, then pours wine with water into the chalice and consecrates it. He says only the part of the institution narrative related to the consecration of the chalice, without being obliged to consecrate the bread again.

II. SACRED FURNISHINGS IN GENERAL

325. As in the case of the building of churches, so also regarding all sacred furnishings the Church admits the artistic style of each region and accepts those adaptations that are in keeping with the culture and traditions of each people, provided that all fit the purpose for which the sacred furnishings are intended.[135]

In this matter as well, a noble simplicity should be ensured such as is the best companion of genuine art.

326. In the choice of materials for sacred furnishings, besides those which are traditional, others are acceptable if by contemporary standards they are considered to be noble, are durable, and are well suited for sacred use. In the dioceses of the United States of America these materials may include wood, stone, or metal which are solid and appropriate to the purpose for which they are employed.

---

135   Cf. Second Vatican Ecumenical Council, Constitution on the Sacred Liturgy, *Sacrosanctum Concilium*, no. 128.

III. SACRED VESSELS

327. Among the requisites for the celebration of Mass, the sacred vessels are held in special honor, especially the chalice and paten, in which the bread and wine are offered and consecrated, and from which they are consumed.

328. Sacred vessels are to be made from precious metal. If they are made from metal that rusts or from a metal less precious than gold, then ordinarily they should be gilded on the inside.

329. In the dioceses of the United States of America, sacred vessels may also be made from other solid materials that, according to the common estimation in each region, are precious, for example, ebony or other hard woods, provided that such materials are suited to sacred use and do not easily break or deteriorate. This applies to all vessels which hold the hosts, such as the paten, the ciborium, the pyx, the monstrance, and other things of this kind.

330. As regards chalices and other vessels that are intended to serve as receptacles for the Blood of the Lord, they are to have bowls of non-absorbent material. The base, on the other hand, may be made of other solid and worthy materials.

331. For the consecration of hosts, a large paten may appropriately be used; on it is placed the bread for the priest and the deacon as well as for the other ministers and for the faithful.

332. As to the form of the sacred vessels, the artist may fashion them in a manner that is more in keeping with the customs of each region, provided each vessel is suited to the intended liturgical use and is clearly distinguishable from those intended for everyday use.

333. For the blessing of sacred vessels, the rites prescribed in the liturgical books are to be followed.[136]

334. The practice is to be kept of building a sacrarium in the sacristy, into which is poured the water from the purification of sacred vessels and linens (cf. no. 280).

IV. SACRED VESTMENTS

335. In the Church, which is the Body of Christ, not all members have the same office. This variety of offices in the celebration of the Eucharist is shown outwardly by the diversity of sacred vestments, which should therefore be a sign of the office proper to each minister. At the same time, however, the sacred vestments should also contribute to the beauty of the sacred action itself. It is appropriate that the vestments to be worn by priests and deacons, as well as those garments to be worn by lay ministers, be blessed according to the rite described in the Roman Ritual[137] before they are put into liturgical use.

336. The sacred garment common to ordained and instituted ministers of any rank is the alb, to be tied at the waist with a cincture unless it is made so as to fit even without such. Before the alb is put on, should this not completely cover the ordinary clothing at the neck, an amice should be put on. The alb may not be replaced by a surplice, not even over a cassock, on occasions when a chasuble or dalmatic is to be worn or when, according to the norms, only a stole is worn without a chasuble or dalmatic.

---

136   Cf. The Roman Pontifical: *Order of the Dedication of a Church and an Altar, editio typica*, 1984, Chapter 7, Order of the Blessing of a Chalice and a Paten; The Roman Ritual, *Book of Blessings, editio typica*, 1984, Order for the Blessing of Articles for Liturgical Use, nos. 1068-1084.

137   Cf. The Roman Ritual, *Book of Blessings, editio typica*, 1984, Order for the Blessing of Articles for Liturgical Use, no. 1070.

337. The vestment proper to the priest celebrant at Mass and other sacred actions directly connected with Mass is, unless otherwise indicated, the chasuble, worn over the alb and stole.

338. The vestment proper to the deacon is the dalmatic, worn over the alb and stole. The dalmatic may, however, be omitted out of necessity or on account of a lesser degree of solemnity.

339. In the dioceses of the United States of America, acolytes, altar servers, lectors, and other lay ministers may wear the alb or other suitable vesture or other appropriate and dignified clothing.

340. The stole is worn by the priest around his neck and hanging down in front. It is worn by the deacon over his left shoulder and drawn diagonally across the chest to the right side, where it is fastened.

341. The cope is worn by the priest in processions and other sacred actions, in keeping with the rubrics proper to each rite.

342. Regarding the design of sacred vestments, Conferences of Bishops may determine and propose to the Apostolic See adaptations that correspond to the needs and the usages of their regions.[138]

343. In addition to the traditional materials, natural fabrics proper to each region may be used for making sacred vestments; artificial fabrics that are in keeping with the dignity of the sacred action and the person wearing them may also be used. The Conference of Bishops will be the judge in this matter.[139]

344. It is fitting that the beauty and nobility of each vestment derive not from abundance of overly lavish ornamentation, but rather from

---

138   Cf. Second Vatican Ecumenical Council, Constitution on the Sacred Liturgy, *Sacrosanctum Concilium*, no. 128.
139   Cf. Second Vatican Ecumenical Council, Constitution on the Sacred Liturgy, *Sacrosanctum Concilium*, no. 128.

the material that is used and from the design. Ornamentation on vestments should, moreover, consist of figures, that is, of images or symbols, that evoke sacred use, avoiding thereby anything unbecoming.

345. The purpose of a variety in the color of the sacred vestments is to give effective expression even outwardly to the specific character of the mysteries of faith being celebrated and to a sense of Christian life's passage through the course of the liturgical year.

346. As to the color of sacred vestments, the traditional usage is to be retained: namely,

    a. White is used in the Offices and Masses during the Easter and Christmas seasons; also on celebrations of the Lord other than of his Passion, of the Blessed Virgin Mary, of the Holy Angels, and of Saints who were not Martyrs; on the Solemnities of All Saints (November 1) and of the Nativity of St. John the Baptist (June 24); and on the Feasts of St. John the Evangelist (December 27), of the Chair of St. Peter (February 22), and of the Conversion of St. Paul (January 25).

    b. Red is used on Palm Sunday of the Lord's Passion and on Good Friday, on Pentecost Sunday, on celebrations of the Lord's Passion, on the feasts of the Apostles and Evangelists, and on celebrations of Martyr Saints.

    c. Green is used in the Offices and Masses of Ordinary Time.

    d. Violet or purple is used in Advent and Lent. It may also be worn in Offices and Masses for the Dead (cf. below).

    e. Besides violet, white or black vestments may be worn at funeral services and at other Offices and Masses for the Dead in the dioceses of the United States of America.

    f. Rose may be used, where it is the practice, on *Gaudete* Sunday (Third Sunday of Advent) and on *Laetare* Sunday (Fourth Sunday of Lent).

    g. On more solemn days, sacred vestments may be used that are festive, that is, more precious, even if not of the color of the day.

h.   Gold- or silver-colored vestments may be worn on more solemn occasions in the dioceses of the United States of America.

347. Ritual Masses are celebrated in their proper color, in white, or in a festive color; Masses for Various Needs, on the other hand, are celebrated in the color proper to the day or the season or in violet if they are of a penitential character, for example, in the *Roman Missal*, no. 31 (in Time of War or Conflict), no. 33 (in Time of Famine), or no. 38 (for the Forgiveness of Sins); Votive Masses are celebrated in the color suited to the Mass itself or even in the color proper to the day or the season.

V. OTHER THINGS INTENDED FOR CHURCH USE

348. Besides sacred vessels and sacred vestments for which some special material is prescribed, other furnishings that either are intended for strictly liturgical use[140] or are in any other way admitted into a church should be worthy and suited to their particular purpose.

349. In a special way, care must be taken that the liturgical books, particularly the *Book of the Gospels* and the Lectionary, which are intended for the proclamation of the word of God and hence enjoy special veneration, really serve in a liturgical action as signs and symbols of heavenly realities and hence are truly worthy, dignified, and beautiful.

350. Furthermore, great attention is to be paid to whatever is directly associated with the altar and the Eucharistic celebration, e.g., the altar cross and the cross carried in procession.

351. Every effort should be made to ensure that even as regards objects of lesser importance the canons of art be appropriately taken into account and that noble simplicity come together with elegance.

---

140   For blessing objects that are designed for liturgical use in churches, cf. The Roman Ritual, *Book of Blessings, editio typica*, 1984, part III.

CHAPTER VII
The Choice of the
Mass and Its Parts

352. The pastoral effectiveness of a celebration will be greatly increased if the texts of the readings, the prayers, and the liturgical songs correspond as closely as possible to the needs, spiritual preparation, and culture of those taking part. This is achieved by appropriate use of the wide options described below.

The priest, therefore, in planning the celebration of Mass, should have in mind the common spiritual good of the people of God, rather than his own inclinations. He should, moreover, remember that the selection of different parts is to be made in agreement with those who have some role in the celebration, including the faithful, in regard to the parts that more directly pertain to each.

Since, indeed, a variety of options is provided for the different parts of the Mass, it is necessary for the deacon, the lectors, the psalmist, the cantor, the commentator, and the choir to be completely sure before the celebration about those texts for which each is responsible is to be used and that nothing be improvised. Harmonious planning and carrying out of the rites will be of great assistance in disposing the faithful to participate in the Eucharist.

I. THE CHOICE OF MASS

353. On solemnities the priest is bound to follow the calendar of the church where he is celebrating.

354. On Sundays, on the weekdays of the Advent, Christmas, Lenten, and Easter Seasons, on feasts, and on obligatory memorials:

a. If Mass is celebrated with a congregation, the priest should follow the calendar of the church where he is celebrating;

b. If Mass is celebrated with the participation of one minister only, the priest may choose either the calendar of the church or his own proper calendar.

355. On optional memorials,

a. On the weekdays of Advent from December 17 to December 24, on days within the Octave of Christmas, and on the weekdays of Lent, except Ash Wednesday and during Holy Week, the Mass for the current liturgical day is to be used; but the collect may be taken from a memorial which happens to be listed in the General Calendar for that day, except on Ash Wednesday and during Holy Week. On weekdays of the Easter Season, memorials of Saints may rightly be celebrated fully.

b. On the weekdays of Advent before December 17, the weekdays of the Christmas Season from January 2, and the weekdays of the Easter Season, it is possible to choose either the weekday Mass, or the Mass of the Saint, or the Mass of one of the Saints whose memorial is observed, or the Mass of any Saint listed in the Martyrology for that day.

c. On the weekdays in Ordinary Time, it is possible to choose either a weekday Mass, or the Mass of an optional memorial which happens to occur on that day, or the Mass of any Saint listed in the Martyrology for that day, or a Mass for Various Needs, or a Votive Mass.

If he celebrates with a congregation, the priest will take care not to omit the readings assigned for each day in the Lectionary for weekdays too frequently and without sufficient reason, since the Church desires that a richer portion at the table of God's word be provided for the faithful.[141]

For the same reason he should use Masses for the Dead in moderation, since every Mass is offered for both the living and the dead, and there is a commemoration of the dead in the Eucharistic Prayer.

Where, however, the optional memorials of the Blessed Virgin Mary or of the Saints are dear to the faithful, the priest should satisfy their legitimate devotion.

When, on the other hand, the option is given of choosing between a memorial found in the General Calendar and one found in a diocesan or religious calendar, preference should be given, all things being equal and in keeping with tradition, to the memorial inscribed in the particular calendar.

II. THE CHOICE OF MASS TEXTS

356. In the choice of texts for the several parts of the Mass, whether of the Season or of the Saints, the following norms should be observed.

The Readings

357. For Sundays and solemnities, three readings are assigned: that is, from a Prophet, an Apostle, and a Gospel. By these the Christian people are brought to know the continuity of the work of salvation according to God's wonderful plan. These readings should be followed strictly. During the Easter Season, according to the tradition of the Church, instead of the reading from the Old Testament, the reading is taken from the Acts of the Apostles.

---

141   Cf. Second Vatican Ecumenical Council, Constitution on the Sacred Liturgy, *Sacrosanctum Concilium*, no. 51.

For feasts, on the other hand, two readings are assigned. If, however, according to the norms a feast is raised to the rank of a solemnity, a third reading is added, taken from the Common.

For memorials of Saints, unless strictly proper readings are given, the readings assigned for the weekday are customarily used. In certain cases, readings are provided that highlight some particular aspect of the spiritual life or activity of the Saint. The use of such readings is not to be insisted upon, unless a pastoral reason suggests it.

358. In the Lectionary for weekdays, readings are provided for each day of every week throughout the entire year; as a result, these readings are for the most part to be used on the days to which they are assigned, unless there occurs a solemnity, feast, or memorial that has its own proper New Testament readings, that is to say, readings in which mention is made of the Saint being celebrated.

If, however, the continuous reading during the week is interrupted by the occurrence of some solemnity or feast, or some particular celebration, then the priest, taking into consideration the entire week's scheme of readings, is allowed either to combine parts omitted with other readings or to decide which readings are to be preferred over others.

In Masses with special groups, the priest is allowed to choose texts more suited to the particular celebration, provided they are taken from the texts of an approved lectionary.

359. In addition, the Lectionary has a special selection of texts from Sacred Scripture for Ritual Masses into which certain Sacraments or Sacramentals are incorporated, or for Masses that are celebrated for certain needs.

Selections of readings of this kind have been established in this way, so that through a more apt hearing of the word of God the faithful may be led to a fuller understanding of the mystery in which they are participating and may be brought to a more ardent love of the word of God.

As a result, texts spoken in the celebration are to be chosen keeping in mind both a suitable pastoral reason and the options allowed in this matter.

360. At times, a longer and shorter form of the same text is given. In choosing between these two forms, a pastoral criterion must be kept in mind. At such times, attention should be paid to the capacity of the faithful to listen with understanding to a reading of greater or lesser length, and to their capacity to hear a more complete text, which is then explained in the homily.[142]

361. When a choice is allowed between alternative texts, whether they are fixed or optional, attention must be paid to what is in the best interests of those taking part, whether it is a matter of using the easier text or one more appropriate in a given group, or of repeating or setting aside a text that is assigned as proper to some particular celebration while being optional for another,[143] as pastoral advantage may suggest.

Such a situation may arise when the same text would have to be read again within a few days, as, for example, on a Sunday and on a following weekday, or when it is feared that a certain text might create some difficulties for a particular group of the Christian faithful. Care should, however, be taken that, when choosing scriptural passages, parts of Sacred Scripture are not permanently excluded.

362. The adaptations to the *Ordo Lectionum Missae* as contained in the Lectionary for Mass for use in the dioceses of the United States of America should be carefully observed.

---

142   *The Roman Missal, Lectionary for Mass, editio typica altera*, 1981, Introduction, no. 80.

143   *The Roman Missal, Lectionary for Mass, editio typica altera*, 1981, Introduction, no. 81.

The Orations

363. In any Mass the orations proper to that Mass are used, unless otherwise noted.

On memorials of Saints, the collect proper to the day is used or, if none is available, one from an appropriate Common. The prayer over the offerings, however, and the prayer after Communion, unless they are proper, may be taken either from the Common or from the weekdays of the current Season.

On the weekdays in Ordinary Time, however, besides the orations from the previous Sunday, orations from another Sunday in Ordinary Time may be used, or one of the prayers for various needs provided in the Missal. It is always permissible, however, to use the collect alone from these Masses.

In this way a richer collection of texts is available, by which the prayer life of the faithful is more abundantly nourished.

During the more important seasons of the year, however, the proper seasonal orations appointed for each weekday in the Missal already make provision for this.

The Eucharistic Prayer

364. The purpose of the many prefaces that enrich the *Roman Missal* is to bring out more fully the motives for thanksgiving within the Eucharistic Prayer and to set out more clearly the different facets of the mystery of salvation.

365. The choice among the Eucharistic Prayers found in the Order of Mass is suitably guided by the following norms:

a. Eucharistic Prayer I, that is, the Roman Canon, which may always be used, is especially suited to be sung or said on days when there is a proper text for the *Communicantes* (*In union with the whole Church*) or in Masses endowed with a proper form of the *Hanc igitur* (*Father, accept this offering*) and also in the celebrations of the Apostles and of the Saints mentioned in the Prayer itself; it is likewise especially appropriate for Sundays, unless for pastoral considerations Eucharistic Prayer III is preferred.

b. Eucharistic Prayer II, on account of its particular features, is more appropriately used on weekdays or in special circumstances. Although it has been provided with its own Preface, it may also be used with other Prefaces, especially those that summarize the mystery of salvation, such as the common Prefaces. When Mass is celebrated for a particular dead person, the special formula may be inserted in the place indicated, namely, before the *Memento etiam* (*Remember our brothers and sisters*).

c. Eucharistic Prayer III may be said with any Preface. Its use is preferred on Sundays and feast days. If, however, this Eucharistic Prayer is used in Masses for the Dead, the special formula for the dead may be used, to be included at the proper place, namely, after the *Omnes filios tuos ubique dispersos, tibi, clemens Pater, miseratus coniunge* (*In mercy and love unite all your children*).

d. Eucharistic Prayer IV has an invariable Preface and gives a fuller summary of salvation history. It may be used when a Mass has no Preface of its own and on Sundays in Ordinary Time. Because of its structure, no special formula for the dead may be inserted into this prayer.

The Chants

366. It is not permitted to substitute other chants for those found in the Order of Mass, such as at the *Agnus Dei*.

367. The norms laid down in their proper places are to be observed for the choice of the chants between the readings, as well as of the chants at the entrance, at the offertory, and at Communion (cf. nos. 40-41, 47-48, 61-64, 74, 86-88).

CHAPTER VIII
Masses and Prayers for Various Circumstances and Masses for the Dead

I. MASSES AND PRAYERS FOR VARIOUS CIRCUMSTANCES

368. Since the liturgy of the Sacraments and Sacramentals causes, for the faithful who are properly disposed, almost every event in life to be sanctified by divine grace that flows from the paschal mystery,[144] and because the Eucharist is the Sacrament of Sacraments, the Missal provides formularies for Masses and orations that may be used in the various circumstances of Christian life, for the needs of the whole world or for the needs of the Church, whether universal or local.

369. In view of the rather broad range of choice among the readings and orations, it is best if Masses for various circumstances be used in moderation, that is, when the occasion truly requires.

370. In all the Masses for various circumstances, unless otherwise expressly indicated, it is permissible to use the weekday readings and also the chants between them, if they are suited to the celebration.

371. Among Masses of this kind are included Ritual Masses, Masses for Various Needs, Masses for Various Circumstances, and Votive Masses.

---

144   Cf. Second Vatican Ecumenical Council, Constitution on the Sacred Liturgy, *Sacrosanctum Concilium*, no. 61.

372. Ritual Masses are connected to the celebration of certain Sacraments or Sacramentals. They are prohibited on Sundays of Advent, Lent, and Easter, on solemnities, on the days within the Octave of Easter, on the Commemoration of All the Faithful Departed (All Souls' Day), on Ash Wednesday, and during Holy Week, taking due account of the norms given in the ritual books or in the Masses themselves.

373. Masses for Various Needs or Masses for Various Circumstances are used in certain situations either as matters arise or at fixed times.

Days or periods of prayer for the fruits of the earth, prayer for human rights and equality, prayer for world justice and peace, and penitential observances outside Lent are to be observed in the dioceses of the United States of America at times to be designated by the diocesan Bishop.

In all the dioceses of the United States of America, January 22 (or January 23, when January 22 falls on a Sunday) shall be observed as a particular day of penance for violations to the dignity of the human person committed through acts of abortion, and of prayer for the full restoration of the legal guarantee of the right to life. The Mass "For Peace and Justice" (no. 22 of the "Masses for Various Needs") should be celebrated with violet vestments as an appropriate liturgical observance for this day.

374. In cases of serious need or pastoral advantage, at the direction of the diocesan Bishop or with his permission, an appropriate Mass may be celebrated on any day except solemnities, the Sundays of Advent, Lent, and Easter, days within the Octave of Easter, the Commemoration of All the Faithful Departed (All Souls' Day), Ash Wednesday, and Holy Week.

375. Votive Masses of the mysteries of the Lord or in honor of the Blessed Virgin Mary or of the Angels or of any given Saint or of all the Saints may be said for the sake of the faithful's devotion on weekdays in Ordinary Time, even if an optional memorial occurs. It is not, however, allowed to celebrate as Votive Masses, those that refer to mysteries related to events in the life of the Lord or of the Blessed Virgin Mary, with the exception of the Mass of the Immaculate Conception, since their celebration is an integral part of the unfolding of the liturgical year.

376. On obligatory memorials, on the weekdays of Advent up to and including December 16, of the Christmas Season from January 2, and of the Easter Season after the Octave of Easter, Masses for Various Needs, Masses for Various Circumstances, and Votive Masses are as such forbidden. If, however, required by some real need or pastoral advantage, according to the judgment of the rector of the church or the priest celebrant himself, a Mass corresponding to such a need or advantage may be used in a celebration with a congregation.

377. On weekdays in Ordinary Time when there is an optional memorial or the Office is of the weekday, it is permissible to use any Mass or oration for various circumstances, though not from the Ritual Masses.

378. It is especially recommended to celebrate the commemoration of the Blessed Virgin Mary on Saturday, because it is to the Mother of the Redeemer in the Liturgy of the Church that in the first place and before all the Saints veneration is given.[145]

---

145   Cf. Second Vatican Ecumenical Council, Dogmatic Constitution on the Church, *Lumen gentium*, no. 54; Paul VI, Apostolic Exhortation *Marialis cultus*, 2 February 1974, no. 9: AAS 66 (1974), pp. 122-123.

II. MASSES FOR THE DEAD

379. The Church offers the Eucharistic Sacrifice of Christ's Passover for the dead so that, since all the members of Christ's body are in communion with each other, the petition for spiritual help on behalf of some may bring comforting hope to others.

380. Among the Masses for the Dead, the Funeral Mass holds first place. It may be celebrated on any day except for solemnities that are holy days of obligation, Holy Thursday, the Easter Triduum, and the Sundays of Advent, Lent, and Easter, with due regard also for all the other requirements of the norm of the law.[146]

381. A Mass for the Dead may be celebrated on receiving the news of a death, for the final burial, or the first anniversary, even on days within the Octave of Christmas, on obligatory memorials, and on weekdays, except for Ash Wednesday or weekdays during Holy Week.

Other Masses for the Dead, that is, "daily" Masses, may be celebrated on weekdays in Ordinary Time on which optional memorials occur or when the Office is of the weekday, provided such Masses are actually applied for the dead.

382. At the Funeral Mass there should, as a rule, be a short homily, but never a eulogy of any kind.

383. The faithful, and especially the family of the deceased, should be urged to participate in the Eucharistic Sacrifice offered for the deceased person also by receiving Holy Communion.

---

146   Cf. particularly *Codex Iuris Canonici*, can. 1176-1185; The Roman Ritual, *Order of Christian Funerals, editio typica*, 1969.

384. If the Funeral Mass is directly joined to the burial rite, once the prayer after Communion has been said and omitting the concluding rite, the rite of final commendation or farewell takes place. This rite is celebrated only if the body is present.

385. In the arranging and choosing of the variable parts of the Mass for the Dead, especially the Funeral Mass (e.g., orations, readings, Prayer of the Faithful), pastoral considerations bearing upon the deceased, the family, and those attending should rightly be taken into account.

Pastors should, moreover, take into special account those who are present at a liturgical celebration or who hear the Gospel on the occasion of the funeral and who may be non-Catholics or Catholics who never or rarely participate in the Eucharist or who seem even to have lost the faith. For priests are ministers of Christ's Gospel for all.

CHAPTER IX
Adaptations Within the Competence of Bishops and Bishops' Conferences

386. The renewal of the *Roman Missal*, carried out in our time in accordance with the decrees of the Second Vatican Ecumenical Council, has taken great care that all the faithful may engage in the celebration of the Eucharist with that full, conscious, and active participation that is required by the nature of the Liturgy itself and to which the faithful, in virtue of their status as such, have a right and duty.[147]

In order, however, to enable such a celebration to correspond all the more fully to the norms and the spirit of the sacred Liturgy, certain further adaptations are set forth in this Instruction and in the Order of Mass and entrusted to the judgment either of the diocesan Bishop or of the Bishops' Conferences.

387. The diocesan Bishop, who is to be regarded as the high priest of his flock, and from whom the life in Christ of the faithful under his care in a certain sense derives and upon whom it depends,[148] must promote, regulate, and be vigilant over the liturgical life in his diocese. It is to him that in this Instruction is entrusted the regulating of the discipline of concelebration (cf. nos. 202, 374) and the establishing of norms regarding the function of serving the priest at the altar (cf. no. 107), the distribution of Holy Communion under both kinds (cf. no. 283), and the

---

147 Cf. Second Vatican Ecumenical Council, Constitution on the Sacred Liturgy, *Sacrosanctum Concilium*, no. 14.

148 Cf. Second Vatican Ecumenical Council, Constitution on the Sacred Liturgy, *Sacrosanctum Concilium*, no. 41.

construction and ordering of churches (cf. no. 291). With him lies responsibility above all for fostering the spirit of the sacred Liturgy in the priests, deacons, and faithful.

388. The adaptations spoken of below that call for a wider degree of coordination are to be decided, in accord with the norm of law, by the Conference of Bishops.

389. It is the competence of the Conferences of Bishops in the first place to prepare and approve an edition of this *Roman Missal* in the authorized vernacular languages, for use in the regions under their care, once their decisions have been accorded the recognitio of the Apostolic See.[149]

The *Roman Missal*, whether in Latin or in lawfully approved vernacular translations, is to be published in its entirety.

390. It is up to the Conferences of Bishops to decide on the adaptations indicated in this General Instruction and in the Order of Mass and, once their decisions have been accorded the recognitio of the Apostolic See, to introduce them into the Missal itself. These adaptations include

- The gestures and posture of the faithful (cf. no. 43);
- The gestures of veneration toward the altar and the *Book of the Gospels* (cf. no. 273);
- The texts of the chants at the entrance, at the presentation of the gifts, and at Communion (cf. nos. 48, 74, 87);
- The readings from Sacred Scripture to be used in special circumstances (cf. no. 362);
- The form of the gesture of peace (cf. no. 82);
- The manner of receiving Holy Communion (cf. nos. 160, 283);

---

149   Cf. *Codex Iuris Canonici*, can. 838 § 3.

- The materials for the altar and sacred furnishings, especially the sacred vessels, and also the materials, form, and color of the liturgical vestments (cf. nos. 301, 326, 329, 339, 342-346).

Directories or pastoral instructions that the Conferences of Bishops judge useful may, with the prior *recognitio* of the Apostolic See, be included in the *Roman Missal* at an appropriate place.

391. It is up to the Conferences of Bishops to provide for the translations of the biblical texts used in the celebration of Mass, exercising special care in this. For it is out of the Sacred Scripture that the readings are read and explained in the homily and that psalms are sung, and it is drawing upon the inspiration and spirit of Sacred Scripture that prayers, orations, and liturgical songs are fashioned in such a way that from them actions and signs derive their meaning.[150]

Language should be used that can be grasped by the faithful and that is suitable for public proclamation, while maintaining those characteristics that are proper to the different ways of speaking used in the biblical books.

392. It will also be up to the Conferences of Bishops to prepare, by means of careful study, a translation of the other texts, so that, even though the character of each language is respected, the meaning of the original Latin text is fully and faithfully rendered. In accomplishing this task, it is expedient to take account of the different literary genres used at Mass, such as the presidential prayers, the antiphons, the acclamations, the responses, the litanies of supplication, and so on.

It should be borne in mind that the primary purpose of the translation of the texts is not with a view to meditation, but rather that they be proclaimed or sung during an actual celebration.

---

150   Cf. Second Vatican Ecumenical Council, Constitution on the Sacred Liturgy, *Sacrosanctum Concilium*, no. 24.

Language should be used that is accommodated to the faithful of the region, but is noble and marked by literary quality, and there will always remain the need for some catechesis on the biblical and Christian meaning of certain words and expressions.

It is, indeed, of advantage that in regions using the same language, the same translation be used whenever possible for liturgical texts, especially for biblical texts and for the Order of Mass.[151]

393. Bearing in mind the important place that singing has in a celebration as a necessary or integral part of the Liturgy,[152] all musical settings of the texts for the people's responses and acclamations in the Order of Mass and for special rites that occur in the course of the liturgical year must be submitted to the Secretariat for the Liturgy of the United States Conference of Catholic Bishops for review and approval prior to publication.

While the organ is to be accorded pride of place, other wind, stringed, or percussion instruments may be used in liturgical services in the dioceses of the United States of America, according to longstanding local usage, provided they are truly apt for sacred use or can be rendered apt.

394. Each diocese should have its own Calendar and Proper of Masses. For its part, the Bishops' Conference should draw up a proper calendar for the nation or, together with other Conferences, a calendar for a wider territory, to be approved by the Apostolic See.[153]

---

151 Cf. Second Vatican Ecumenical Council, Constitution on the Sacred Liturgy, *Sacrosanctum Concilium*, no. 36:3.
152 Cf. Second Vatican Ecumenical Council, Constitution on the Sacred Liturgy, *Sacrosanctum Concilium*, no. 112.
153 Cf. *General Norms for the Liturgical Year and the Calendar*, nos. 48-51, p. 99; Sacred Congregation for Divine Worship, Instruction *Calendaria particularia*, 24 June 1970, nos. 4, 8: AAS 62 (1970), pp. 652-653.

In carrying this out, to the greatest extent possible the Lord's Day is to be preserved and safeguarded, as the primordial holy day, and hence other celebrations, unless they be truly of the greatest importance, should not have precedence over it.[154] Care should likewise be taken that the liturgical year as revised by decree of the Second Vatican Council not be obscured by secondary elements.

In the drawing up of the calendar of a nation, the Rogation and Ember Days should be indicated (cf. no. 373), as well as the forms and texts for their celebration,[155] and other special measures should also be taken into consideration.

It is appropriate that in publishing the Missal, celebrations proper to an entire nation or territory be inserted at the correct place among the celebrations of the General Calendar, while those proper to a region or diocese be placed in a special appendix.

395. Finally, if the participation of the faithful and their spiritual welfare require variations and more thoroughgoing adaptations in order that the sacred celebration respond to the culture and traditions of the different peoples, then Bishops' Conferences may propose such to the Apostolic See in accordance with article 40 of the *Constitution on the Sacred Liturgy* for introduction with the latter's consent, especially in the case

---

154   Cf. Second Vatican Ecumenical Council, Constitution on the Sacred Liturgy, *Sacrosanctum Concilium*, no. 106.
155   Cf. *General Norms for the Liturgical Year and Calendar*, no. 46, p. 98; cf. also Sacred Congregation for Divine Worship, Instruction *Calendaria particularia*, 24 June 1970, no. 38: AAS 62 (1970), p. 660.

of peoples to whom the Gospel has been more recently proclaimed.[156] The special norms given in the *Instruction On the Roman Liturgy and Inculturation*[157] should be carefully observed.

Regarding procedures to be followed in this matter, the following should be followed:

In the first place, a detailed preliminary proposal should be set before the Apostolic See, so that, after the necessary faculty has been granted, the detailed working out of the individual points of adaptation may proceed.

Once these proposals have been duly approved by the Apostolic See, experiments should be carried out for specified periods and at specified places. If need be, once the period of experimentation is concluded, the Bishops' Conference shall decide upon pursuing the adaptations and shall propose a mature formulation of the matter to the Apostolic See for its decision.[158]

396. Before, however, proceeding to new adaptations, especially those more thoroughgoing, great care should be taken to promote the proper instruction of clergy and faithful in a wise and orderly fashion, so as to take advantage of the faculties already foreseen and to implement fully the pastoral norms concerning the spirit of a celebration.

---

156   Cf. Second Vatican Ecumenical Council, Constitution on the Sacred Liturgy, *Sacrosanctum Concilium*, nos. 37-40.

157   Cf. Congregation for Divine Worship and the Discipline of the Sacraments, Instruction *Varietates legitimae*, 25 January 1994, nos. 54, 62-69: AAS 87 (1995), pp. 308-309, 311-313.

158   Cf. Congregation for Divine Worship and the Discipline of the Sacraments, Instruction *Varietates legitimae*, 25 January 1994, nos. 66-68: AAS 87 (1995), p. 313.

397. Furthermore, the principle shall be respected according to which each particular Church must be in accord with the universal Church not only regarding the doctrine of the faith and sacramental signs, but also as to the usages universally handed down by apostolic and unbroken tradition. These are to be maintained not only so that errors may be avoided, but also so that the faith may be passed on in its integrity, since the Church's rule of prayer (*lex orandi*) corresponds to her rule of belief (*lex credendi*).[159]

The Roman Rite constitutes a notable and precious part of the liturgical treasure and patrimony of the Catholic Church. Its riches are of benefit to the universal Church, so that were they to be lost, the Church would be seriously harmed.

Throughout the ages, the Roman Rite has not only preserved the liturgical usages that arose in the city of Rome, but has also in a deep, organic, and harmonious way incorporated into itself certain other usages derived from the customs and culture of different peoples and of various particular Churches of both West and East, so that in this way, the Roman Rite has acquired a certain supraregional character. In our own times, on the other hand, the identity and unitary expression of this Rite is found in the typical editions of the liturgical books promulgated by authority of the Supreme Pontiff, and in those liturgical books corresponding to them approved by the Bishops' Conferences for their territories with the *recognitio* of the Apostolic See.[160]

---

159   Cf. Congregation for Divine Worship and the Discipline of the Sacraments, Instruction *Varietates legitimae*, 25 January 1994, nos. 26-27: AAS 87 (1995), pp. 298-299.
160   Cf. John Paul II, Apostolic Letter *Vicesimus Quintus Annus*, 4 December 1988, no. 16: AAS 81 (1989), p. 912; Congregation for Divine Worship and the Discipline of the Sacraments, Instruction *Varietates legitimae*, 25 January 1994, nos. 2, 36: AAS 87 (1995), pp. 288, 302.

398. The norm established by the Second Vatican Council—that in the liturgical reform there should be no innovations unless required in order to bring a genuine and certain benefit to the Church, and taking care that any new forms adopted should in some way grow organically from forms already existing[161]—must also be applied to efforts at the inculturation of the same Roman Rite.[162] Inculturation, moreover, requires a necessary length of time, lest the authentic liturgical tradition suffer contamination due to haste and a lack of caution.

Finally, the purpose of pursuing inculturation is not in any way the creation of new families of rites, but aims rather at meeting the needs of a particular culture in such a way that adaptations introduced either in the Missal or in combination with other liturgical books are not at variance with the distinctive character of the Roman Rite.[163]

399. And so, the *Roman Missal*, even if in different languages and with some variety of customs,[164] must be preserved in the future as an instrument and an outstanding sign of the integrity and unity of the Roman Rite.[165]

---

161 Cf. Second Vatican Ecumenical Council, Constitution on the Sacred Liturgy, *Sacrosanctum Concilium*, no. 23.
162 Cf. Congregation for Divine Worship and the Discipline of the Sacraments, Instruction *Varietates legitimae*, 25 January 1994, no. 46: AAS 87 (1995), p. 306.
163 Cf. Congregation for Divine Worship and the Discipline of the Sacraments, Instruction *Varietates legitimae*, 25 January 1994, no. 36: AAS 87 (1995), p. 302.
164 Cf. Congregation for Divine Worship and the Discipline of the Sacraments, Instruction *Varietates legitimae*, 25 January 1994, no. 54: AAS 87 (1995), pp. 308-309.
165 Cf. Second Vatican Ecumenical Council, Constitution on the Sacred Liturgy, *Sacrosanctum Concilium*, no. 38; Paul VI, Apostolic Constitution *Missale Romanum*, p. 14.

Index to the
General Instruction of
the Roman Missal

Church	1, 2, 3, 5, 9, 10, 11, 12, 15, 16, 17, 18, 19, 20, 22, 27, 29, 33, 45, 50, 53, 54, 55, 66, 69, 70, 72, 73, 75, 79, 82, 91, 92, 93, 94, 105, 106, 107, 111, 112, 113, 140, 149, 199, 202, 203, 210, 220, 228, 282, 283, 288, 289, 290, 292, 293, 294, 295, 298, 301, 303, 309, 311, 312, 314, 315, 318, 319, 320, 325, 335, 348, 353, 354, 355, 357, 365, 368, 376, 378, 379, 387, 397, 398; Notes 2, 22, 78, 81, 93, 133, 136, 140, 145
Ciborium	160, 163, 306, 329
Cincture	119, 336
Civil authorities	69
Clergy	310, 396
Collect	30, 43, 45, 46, 48, (Heading before) 54, 54, 127, 128, 259, 261, 355, 363
Collection	48, 56, 61, 87, 105, 363
Colors	304, 346
Commentator	105, 352
Communication	310
Communion	5, 13, 14, 30, 33, 34, 37, 43, 44, 45, 46., 72, 79, (Heading before) 80, 80, 82, 83, (Heading before) 84, 85, 86, 87, 88, 89, 100, 118, 154, 156, 159, 160, 161, 162, 163, 165, 166, 171, 182, 183, 184, 191, 192, 198, (Heading before) 237, 240, 242, 246, 248, 249, 267, 268, 269, 271, 274, 278, 279, (Heading before) 281, 281, 282, 283, 284, 285, 286, 287, 311, 321, 324, 363, 367, 379, 383, 384, 387, 390; Notes 98, 106, 107, 126, 129, 130
Communion antiphon	87, 269

Saint	6, 7, 8, 1539, 61, 275, 277, 302, 3118, 346, 355, 356, 357, 358, 363, 365, 375, 378; Note 48
Salvation	2, 5, 19, 55, 57, 69, 70, 72, 79, 83, 93, 282, 357, 364, 365
Seat	207, 246, 250, 294, 310, 311
Sequence	64, 70
Service	307, 346, 393
Sign of Peace	82, 83, 154, 181, 239, 266
Silence	43, (Heading before) 45, 45, 51, 54, 55, (Heading before) 56, 56, 66, 71, 78, 128, 130, 136, 147, 164, 165, 271
Sin	347
Singing	32, 38, (Heading before) 39, 39, 40, 43, 48, 55, 61, 74, 86, 87, 96, 102, 103, 104, 114, 115, 132, 151, 175, 198, 313, 393
Species	3, 7, 14, 27, 79, 94, 161, 162, 282, 284
Spiritual life	357
Spoon	245
Stational Mass	203
Stole	92, 119, 209, 336, 337, 338, 340
Sunday	11, 13, 40, 51, 53, 64, 66, 68, 113, 115, 117, 119, 204, 305, 313, 346, 354, 357, 361, 363, 365, 372, 373, 374, 380
Symbol	67, 288, 301, 344, 349
Tabernacle	274, 310, 314, 315, 316; Note 127